ROUTLEDGE LIBRARY EDITIONS: SOVIET SOCIETY

Volume 27

YOUNG SOVIET FILM MAKERS

YOUNG SOVIET FILM MAKERS

JEANNE VRONSKAYA

Foreword by
JOHN GILLETT

LONDON AND NEW YORK

First published in 1972 by George Allen & Unwin Ltd.

This edition first published in 2025
by Routledge
4 Park Square, Milton Park, Abingdon, Oxon OX14 4RN

and by Routledge
605 Third Avenue, New York, NY 10158

Routledge is an imprint of the Taylor & Francis Group, an informa business

© 1972 George Allen & Unwin Ltd.

All rights reserved. No part of this book may be reprinted or reproduced or utilised in any form or by any electronic, mechanical, or other means, now known or hereafter invented, including photocopying and recording, or in any information storage or retrieval system, without permission in writing from the publishers.

Trademark notice: Product or corporate names may be trademarks or registered trademarks, and are used only for identification and explanation without intent to infringe.

British Library Cataloguing in Publication Data
A catalogue record for this book is available from the British Library

ISBN: 978-1-032-86028-2 (Set)
ISBN: 978-1-032-87779-2 (Volume 27) (hbk)
ISBN: 978-1-032-87780-8 (Volume 27) (pbk)
ISBN: 978-1-003-53443-3 (Volume 27) (ebk)

DOI: 10.4324/9781003534433

Publisher's Note
The publisher has gone to great lengths to ensure the quality of this reprint but points out that some imperfections in the original copies may be apparent.

Disclaimer
The publisher has made every effort to trace copyright holders and would welcome correspondence from those they have been unable to trace.

Young Soviet Film Makers

by Jeanne Vronskaya

Foreword by John Gillett

London George Allen and Unwin Ltd
Ruskin House   Museum Street

First Published in 1972

This book is copyright under the Berne Convention.
All rights are reserved. Apart from any fair dealing for the
purpose of private study, research, criticism or review, as
permitted under the Copyright Act, 1956, no part of this
publication may be reproduced, stored in a retrieval system,
or transmitted, in any form or by any means, electronic,
electrical, chemical, mechanical, optical, photocopying,
recording or otherwise, without the prior permission of the
copyright owner. Enquiries should be addressed to the
publishers.

© George Allen & Unwin Ltd. 1972

ISBN 0 04 791023 2 hardback
     0 04 791024 0 paper

Printed in Great Britain
in 10 point Plantin type
by BAS Printers Limited
Wallop, Hampshire

I hope that this small contribution will help readers get a better idea of the work of young Russian film makers today.

Jeanne Vronskaya   1971

TO I.B. IN FONDEST MEMORY

Foreword

Those interested in the development of the Soviet cinema can find several books dealing with its early history—the excitements and experiments of the 1920s (Eisenstein, Dovzhenko, Pudovkin, Kuleshov, Dziga Vertov, Protazanov); the crisis-ridden decade of the thirties with the emergence of social realism and its trail of masterworks and unfinished projects; and the war and immediate post-war periods, full of uncertainties, political polemics, and the infamous Zhdanov decrees on the purpose of art in a socialist society. Before Madame Vronskaya's book, however, we had no detailed study in English of what happened when the Soviet cinema came to life again in the late 1950s; her survey mainly covers developments over the last fifteen years with facts, figures and notes on a host of interesting new talents whom one might call the post-Stalinist generation, artists who are striving to create new styles and methods to reflect the reality of their society *as they see it*.

Of course, there have been many failures during this period and many films which are of interest only to local audiences but it is a fact that, if one looks at production not only in Moscow and Leningrad but in all the regional centres of the USSR, a large body of fascinating work can be uncovered. In this respect, the section of the book devoted to the Asian Republics is particularly relevant and revealing: the Georgian cinema has been active for many years and has recently produced directors like Danelia and Yoseliani whose individual qualities of observation and humour deserve to be widely known in the West.

And here, as they say, is the rub. It is a matter of regret that owing to the ever-changing official Soviet attitudes to their own films, and the tardiness of West European exhibitors and distributors to handle those productions which are made available to them, the majority of the films discussed here are not readily accessible to us. There are signs that some improvements are on the way: Soviet Film Weeks have been held in a number of European capitals and Soviet Embassies often hold films which are not distributed elsewhere. In other words, everything must be done to ensure that works by artists like Tarkovsky, Khutsiev, Mikhalkov-Konchalovsky, Alov and Naumov, Shepitko, Panfilov are properly disseminated abroad, and here we must hope for a little more understanding from the Soviet authorities themselves. To keep major works of art like Tarkovsky's *Andrei Rublev* (and, in another field, Shostakovich's 13th Symphony) under cover for so many years reflects no credit on anyone, as well as being an insult to the artists concerned. Film, unlike theatre or painting, is a relatively easy art to transport from one country to another; let us hope that those responsible in both East and West will realise that both parts of the world are desperately eager to discover what their artists are doing.

Young Soviet Film Makers

This book gives the English reader an intriguing glimpse of the Russian film world as seen from the inside. Madame Vronskaya is an enthusiastic and constructive critic who, despite the strictures in some areas of her survey, clearly has great love and respect for the best manifestations of the Soviet cinema.

JOHN GILLETT

Acknowledgements

The author would like to express her sincere thanks to:
  Mike Wallington
  Vladimir Czugunow
  Douglas Grant
  Irene Trokhimovska
  Dagmar Sarkar
  Michel Arnauld
  Alex Lipkow
for their kindness and help.

Contents

Foreword by John Gillett	page 11	4 COMEDIES	page 51
Acknowledgements	13	The Twenties	51
		The Thirties	51
INTRODUCTION	17	Since the War	53
A Short History	17	After Stalin's Death	53
Fresh Winds	18	Great Comics	56
The VGIK	23		
		5 BOX-OFFICE PICTURES AND ACTORS	60

PART I TOWARDS A NEW CINEMA

PART II CINEMA OF THE NATIONAL MINORITIES

1 THE DEPARTURE FROM SOCIAL REALISM	27
Andrei Tarkovsky	27
Andron Mikhalkov-Konchalovsky	28
Emergence of a New School	29
2 CONTROVERSIAL DIRECTORS	33
Tarkovsky's *Andrei Rublev*	33
Mikhalkov-Konchalovsky's *Asya's Happiness*	36
Elem Klimov's Bitter Satires	36
Larissa Shepitko	38
Western Influence	39
Alexei Saltykov	41
3 YOUNG INTELLECTUALS	42
Mikhail Bogin	42
Pavel Lubimov	44
Alexander Mitta	46
Vladimir Fetin	47
Gleb Panfilov	48
Vassili Shukshin	49

6 EXPERIMENTS IN THE CAUCASUS	65
Historical Outline—Georgia	65
—Armenia	69
—Azerbaidzhan	70
Modern Georgia	70
7 THE LITHUANIAN FILM STUDIO	81
8 MOLDAVIAN CINEMA	87
9 THE AWAKENING OF THE STEPPES	91

PART III

10 APPENDIX I—SOVIET FILM STUDIOS	104
11 APPENDIX II—CHRONOLOGICAL LIST OF MAIN FILMS (1956–72)	106
12 FILMOGRAPHIES	109
13 SELECTED BIBLIOGRAPHY	123
Index	124

Introduction

A Short History

If one calls literature the heart of a society, then the cinema is its face.

It is impossible to discuss art and artistic developments without considering the historical circumstances of the times. This is especially true in Russia, where the political climate necessarily influences culture. During half a century of the Communist regime in Russia many important events and developments have taken place, which have to a greater or lesser extent influenced cinema—the Revolution, the Civil War, collectivisation and industrialisation, the purges in the thirties, the Second World War, the terror of Stalin's last years and his death. All these events found their reflection on the Soviet screen.

The Golden Age of Soviet cinema in the twenties was largely connected with the fact that the impetus of revolutionary enthusiasm, proselytising film as the art *par excellence* for the masses, had not yet been frozen by the new establishment after the recent turmoil of Revolution and Civil War. The rulers, occupied by other things, granted all the arts a great degree of freedom; but the grey oppressiveness of the new bureaucracy was soon to emerge.

By the late twenties the new ruling class had consolidated its position, and after 1928 Soviet film makers hit hard times. In the thirties, the heyday of Stalinism, when people were sent to the Siberian concentration camps in their hundreds of thousands, one of the cinema's leading lights was Pyriev, whose films *The Rich Bride*, *The Tractor Drivers* and *Swineherd and Shepherd* depicted well-fed and round-faced 'stage' villagers in colourful national dress, who spent their time singing or feasting at tables covered with mountains of the choicest food.

The thirties also witnessed the fantastic flowering of the cult of the 'great and beloved' leader. On the eve of the Second World War, Stalin actually appeared, as the main hero, in pseudo-historical films about the revolutionary period, with Lenin shown almost as his apprentice. The terror of these days was partially reflected in the innumerable so-called 'spy films', where the Party again and again preached 'vigilance', drawing attention to imperialist plots which allegedly extended throughout the country and included the most improbable alliances—Trotsky and Hitler, for instance, or British imperialists and reactionary orthodox churchmen. Well-known film makers were coerced into taking part in this 'Black Sabbath'. The situation in the country was so strained that any individual creativity was stifled at the very start and soon became unthinkable. As improbable as it may seem, the situation changed for the better only at the beginning of the Second World War. This was well expressed by Boris Pasternak, who wrote in *Dr Zhivago:* 'And when the war broke out its real horrors, its real dangers, its menace of real death were a blessing compared with the inhuman power of the lie, a relief because it broke the spell of the dead letter.'

The immediate aftermath of the war was probably the most difficult period in the history of Soviet cinema. The film industry was given instructions to 'make masterpieces' only; as a result production literally dried up. Some of the provincial film studios were shut altogether, and the films which were made during these years leave an extremely unpleasant impression.

Taken as a whole, the period from the thirties to Stalin's death was a tragic one for many directors, especially those with great talent. Sergei Eisenstein had to leave many plans unrealised, and his *Ivan the Terrible* (Part II) lay on the shelf for twelve years. Dziga Vertov, who had to work from 1944 till 1954 as an ordinary newsreel editor, died completely forgotten and forsaken by everybody, and Alexander Dovzhenko, whose last film, *Life in Blossom* (1949) was made for the home market, had to make a special 'export' version of this film under the title *Michurin*. In his final years (1949–56) Dovzhenko made no films whatsoever, but wrote scripts and taught at the VGIK*, Vsevolod Pudovkin, too, was obliged to take part in the making of such pathetic, odious biographical films as *Admiral Nakhimov* (1947) and *Zhukovsky* (1950).

Fresh Winds

The young generation of film makers, who began their work in the late fifties, brought about far-reaching changes in the Soviet film industry. New ideas, new styles, new methods suddenly appeared on the screen.

The time was ripe for this revolution of young talent. Indeed, these years can, in some respects, almost be compared with the Golden Age in the twenties.

Both periods displayed creative fervour and high professional skill, although the line of development in the sixties was diametrically opposed to that of the twenties: in contrast to the monumental, social (or collectivist) and politically committed (often unashamedly propagandist) cinema of the twenties, the sixties saw the return of personal themes, analytical thinking, in-depth portraits, and an unparalleled outburst of individual (even consciously individualistic) styles. This does not mean, however, that all taboos have been broken. There are no sex or horror films—good or bad—in the USSR (yet). A political approach overtly contradicting the official line is also impossible.

The long lethargy of Stalin's time was broken by Grigori Chukhrai's film *The Forty First* (1956). The rather belated debut of this gifted director (he was already thirty-five at that time), who has since become an outstanding master of Soviet cinema, received international acclaim, and overnight he became an idol of young film-goers. The movement gathered momentum when two veterans—the director Mikhail Kalatozov and the cameraman, Sergei Urusevsky* (who could be described as the Soviet Raoul Coutard) —made *The Cranes are Flying* (1957), which was to become the symbol and expression of the new epoch. *The Cranes* caused a real sensation at home and Tatyana Samoilova, who played the lead, won the praise of the severest film critics, while at a quite different level the public showed its admiration by making Tanya's slant eyes a fashion to be followed in Moscow and all over Russia.

---

* Moscow Film Institute.

* He was the cameraman on *The Forty First*.

Introduction

After *The Cranes*, distributors in many countries signed up Kalatozov's and Urusevsky's next work *The Letter That Was Not Sent* (1960), even before the film was completed. In the interim, Chukhrai's second film *Ballad of a Soldier*, and a film called *Destiny of a Man*, in which the actor Sergei Bondarchuk made his directorial debut, caused a great stir. The influence of these new-style films on Soviet youth was tremendous. Queues at cinemas became a common sight, and tickets went for three times the normal price.

Two more Soviet films arrived on the international screen in 1960—*The Lady With A Little Dog* by Joseph Heifitz, a director of the older generation, and *Splendid Days* (*Seryozha*) by the young directors, Georgi Danelia and Igor Talankin. In 1961 a glut of interesting films were made—the young director Andrei Tarkovsky and his cameraman, Vadim Yusov, won an award in New York for their short, *The Steam-Roller and the Violin*; Chukhrai, world famous by then, made the anti-Stalinist feature *Clear Skies*, about the tragic fate of a man in totalitarian society; and the old-timer, Mikhail Romm, who in his time had directed many hagiographical films about Lenin, shot an excellent 'intellectual' feature, called *Nine Days in One Year*, which provoked sharp controversy in the Soviet press. It is worth mentioning, that this latter film was the first major success of Innokenti Smoktunovsky, the best Soviet film actor of recent years (probably most widely known in the West as Hamlet in Grigori Kozintsev's screen version of the play).

In the same year Mikhail Kalik, who had spent a number of years in labour camps, shot a lyrical *avant-garde* picture *Man Following the Sun*, which clearly echoes Lamorisse's *Le Ballon Rouge* and is influenced by Matisse, and Saint-Exupéry's book *Le Petit Prince*. Alexander Alov and Vladimir Naumov were awarded the Grand Prix at the Venice Festival for *Peace to the Newcomer*, notable for its brilliant camerawork. The veteran director, Yuli Raizman, somewhat unexpectedly presented a dual treatment of a love theme and the problems of education in his feature *And What If It Is Love?* Also in 1961, Andrei Tarkovsky shot *Ivan's Childhood*, about a child's life marred by war. The film collected four prizes at international film events and Tarkovsky became the leading exponent of *cinéma d'auteur* in contemporary Russia. At the same time, his close friend and script-writer, Andron Mikhalkov-Konchalovsky, also showed himself to be a budding director: he won the Bronze Lion at the Venice Festival for his short colour film *The Boy and the Pigeon*, which again shows Lamorisse's immense popularity in the Russian cinema.

By then this tremendous upsurge of cinematic creativity had reached its height, and one young film maker after another made his debut, while the older directors strove not to fall behind. In 1963 two excellent new directors appeared, Pavel Lubimov and Larissa Shepitko, both graduates of VGIK. Lubimov's short *The Aunt With Violets* and 22-year-old Shepitko's feature *Heat* both made headlines and won international prizes. Next year the 'old men' of cinema recaptured some of the limelight by simultaneously presenting a number of *chef d'oeuvres*: Kozintsev with his version of *Hamlet*, starring Smoktunovsky and Kalatozov and Urusevsky with a feature film *I Am Cuba*. In 1964 Chukhrai made *There Was an Old Man and an Old Woman*, a naturalistic film on contemporary themes (unlike the fairy-tale atmosphere suggested by the title), but it was too long and not up to his usual standard.

In 1964, after a turbulent three years of shooting and re-shooting, the final controversial version of *I Am Twenty* was released. The Georgian-born director, Marlen Khutsiev had made his debut as long ago as

Young Soviet Film Makers

1959 with *The Two Fyodors*, an intimate, human film, whose simplicity and realism became a model and inspiration for many of the younger enthusiasts. *I Am Twenty* was made in the spirit of Italian neo-realism. Elem Klimov even attempted a satire on Soviet society in general and Khrushchev in particular in his film *Welcome*. This comedy was not passed for release, and Soviet cinematography acquired a new term—'shelved films'—a category which by now includes a great many films. Needless to say, 'shelved films' are certainly not the dullest in Soviet cinema.

1965 saw the debut of several more young talents. Mikhail Bogin made a romantic short, *The Two* (at the Riga film studio) and Mikhalkov-Konchalovsky presented as his diploma work the brilliant feature *The First Teacher*. He had learned much from Wajda, but his work was, nevertheless, absolutely fresh and original.

The Armenian, Sergei Paradzhanov and the cameraman Yuri Ilyenko (who has now turned to directing), shot *Shadows of Our Forgotten Ancestors*, a film which collected no fewer than sixteen international prizes from all over the world. Not since Eisenstein's triumphs had Russian cinema enjoyed such international esteem.

By 1966, Joseph Heifitz had made a new adaptation of a Chekhov story: *In the Town of S.;* Sergei Bondarchuk had started on the road which later led him to the monumental *Waterloo*, with the four-part epic *War and Peace*, which took five years to complete; and Marlen Khutsiev continued to develop his ideas on contemporary youth with *Rain in July*, depicting the life of the Soviet intelligentsia with its hopes, desires and frustrations. This year saw the appearance of a very original screen version of Dostoyevsky's short story *Bad Joke* by Alexander Alov and Vladimir Naumov. All previous attempts to bring Dostoyevsky to the screen (Pyriev's adaptations, for example) had been unsuccessful. Alov and Naumov gave the satirical story a contemporary slant. The film failed to get a release. In the same year, Tarkovsky finished *Andrei Rublev*, which had aroused controversies even during shooting and could have remained shelved forever, had it not been awarded the prize of the film critics (FIPRESCI) at the Cannes Festival in 1969. Mikhalkov-Konchalovsky, who co-scripted *Andrei Rublev* with Tarkovsky, and directed *The First Teacher*, has had one of his own films 'shelved'— *Asya's Happiness*, a deceptively simple account of rural life in the Soviet Union today. This film has at last been given a Russian release.

Pavel Lubimov finished his second film *The Women*, a refreshingly frank and human approach to feminine problems. It was a great hit in the Soviet Union and gave Lubimov the reputation of being an 'expert in female psychology'.

Pyotr Todorovsky, a director of the middle generation and a former cameraman, made an interesting feature, *The Enigmatic Indian*, about the life of the Soviet intelligentsia, which was also not released, since the portrayal was too realistic. Todorovsky's first film *Fidelity*, about young soldiers who go to the front at seventeen, won an international prize. Both films show the strong influence of Khutsiev, which is not surprising, since Todorovsky worked as Khutsiev's cameraman on the first feature of this pioneer neo-realist.

In 1969 Mikhalkov-Konchalovsky presented an original and visually stunning adaptation of Ivan Turgenev's novel *A Nest of Gentlefolk*, which will surely remain a classic in its own genre. After that he made a screen version of Chekhov's *Uncle Vanya* (1970) with Sergei Bondarchuk and Innokenti Smoktunovsky in the main roles.

Introduction

Nova), a film about the life of the eighteenth-century Armenian poet Sayat Nova, who was killed during a Persian invasion. Paradzhanov's former cameraman, the Ukrainian Yuri Ilyenko, made *On the Eve of Ivan Kupala Day* (based on Gogol's fantastic stories), under the influence of Dovzhenko. The Georgians, Tengiz Abuladze and Alexander Kveselava translated the poems of the Georgian classical writer Vazha Pshavela into dazzling images.

The sixties produced a very interesting group of

Uncle Vanya by Andron Mikhalkov-Konchalovsky (Sergei Bondarchuk and Innokenti Smoktunovsky as Uncle Vanya)

Igor Talankin made a biographical colour version of *Tchaikovsky*, which would be beautiful, were it not for the pedestrian style and routine realism. According to Talankin, his film is meant to be 'a glimpse into the creative laboratory, into the inner world of the artist and the heavy burden of genius', but the translation of such schematic statements into screen language is very difficult.

In 1969 films appeared which show a retreat from dogmatic realism and a much more creative approach to the expressive possibilities of film language. Sergei Paradzhanov took the exotic and glittering East as the backcloth for his *Colour of the Pomegranate* (*Sayat*

Tchaikovsky by Igor Talankin with Innokenti Smoktunovsky in the lead

21

Young Soviet Film Makers

young directors from Georgia and the Central Asian Republics. Their industries were very different: Georgia had a solid film making history and rich experience to build upon, while in Central Asia the young film makers had to start from scratch. The most significant of the Georgians are Georgi Danelia, Otar Yoseliani and Mikhail Kobakhidze. Danelia has made *Seryozha, I Walk About Moscow* with master-cameraman Vadim Yusov, *The Thirty Three* (a 'shelved' comedy) and *Cheer Up!* (again with Yusov on camera). Since Danelia is an individualist *par excellence*, he always prefers the sensitive collaboration of Yusov, who seems to understand every nuance of the director's intentions. Yoseliani works in Khutsiev's style. Kobakhidze specialises in short films, which are miniature masterpieces. Both deserve to be more widely known and, no doubt, would have been if they had had more opportunities to show their work abroad.

The Central Asian industry started with Larissa Shepitko's *Heat*. This was the first time that a film of the 'new cinema' was made in Kirghizia. The lead was played by a Kirghiz student, Bolot Shamshiev, who has now graduated from the director's faculty of VGIK and is already a famous film maker in his own right.

Tolomush Okeev, a former film recordist, is another interesting director from Kirghizia. He was responsible for the amazing sound-track on *Heat*, and in five years has made two shorts and three feature films, two of which have won prizes.

Three young Uzbek cinéastes – director Elier Ishmukhamedov, scriptwriter Odelsha Agishev, and cameraman Dilshat Fatkhullin – usually work together. Fatkhullin, especially, shows great promise. He shot Ishmukhamedov's *Tenderness*, a film singled out for international awards.

In 1971 a number of interesting films reached the

Colour of the Pomegranate (Sayat Nova) by Sergei Paradzhanov

screen, including a few screen versions of Chekhov— *The Merry-go-round* after short stories from note books, made by Mikhail Shveitser and Yuli Karasik's version of *The Seagull;* Yuri Ilyenko's film *White Bird with a Black Spot* about the establishment of Soviet rule in Western Ukraine, and a new comedy, *Day After Day* by Otar Yoseliani were also notable.

Such is the general picture in Soviet cinema today. Despite the great diversity of subjects, tendencies, styles and ideas, we can discern certain general principles which unite this younger generation of Soviet film makers—the rejection of conformist methods and a search for fresh modes of expression; the depiction of life through oblique interrelations and ellipses; a more uninhibited approach to the problems of Soviet society; a tendency towards realism rather than social realism, disregard of old-fashioned narrative and plot structure, and an intensive search for poetic self-expression. In short, we can now see new forms and a new screen language.

The VGIK

The main training ground for all seeking a professional qualification in film in the USSR is the All-Union State Cinematography Institute (the VGIK) in Moscow. The most famous directors were trained here—Chukhrai, Khutsiev, Tarkovsky, Paradzhanov, etc. VGIK has its own small studio, where students can make their own shorts and low budget films. It has seven faculties—directors, cameramen, actors, script-writers, critics, set-designers and managers of film production and film distribution. The history of this famous school of cinematography is worth a mention.

VGIK was founded in 1919. At first the whole school was housed in only four rooms in the building of the First Studio of Moscow Art Theatre (the MHAT): there was only one workshop, with twenty-five people. Later, in the spring of 1920, the number of students rose to 165. What they lost in scale of operation they gained in unbounded enthusiasm: among the pupils at that time were Vsevolod Pudovkin, Boris Barnet, Alexandra Khokhlova, Vladimir Vogel and others. In those early days, the school was often mobile or homeless; there were times when it even had to 'live' in private apartments. No grants were available. The students only received food – some flour and a few salted herrings – which was not to be sniffed at in those hungry times. The school mostly had to manage for itself: the students arranged

The Seagull by Yuli Karasik

performances to earn money for the school and themselves. Konstantin Stanislavsky, Yevgeni Vakhtangov, Vsevolod Meyerhold, as well as Lenin's minister of culture, Lunacharsky, often visited these performances. Among the staff was Vladimir Gardin, an actor and director of great renown, the founder of the school; the lecturers were Lev Kuleshov, a famous stage and screen actress Olga Preobrazhenskaya, an actor from MHAT, Leonid Leonidov, and others. Few films were produced in Russia at that time; and in the conditions of Civil War and the blockade it was almost impossible to obtain stock. Nevertheless, that special enthusiastic spirit triumphed and this unique institution soon became world famous.

From 1919 to 1921 the VGIK made five films: *The*

Young Soviet Film Makers

Iron Heel, a staged version of a novel by Jack London; two propaganda films *In the Days of Struggle*, scripted and directed by I. Perestiani, with V. Pudovkin, and the adventure film *On The Red Front*, scripted and directed by Lev Kuleshov; the film *Hunger – Hunger – Hunger*, scripted and directed by V. Gardin and V. Pudovkin, about the hunger in the Volga region, and the full length serial-feature, *Hammer and Sickle (The Difficult Times)*, by the director V. Gardin and cameraman E. Tisse.

In the early twenties the film school was gradually reorganised, and the number of faculties increased. In 1924, a workshop of directors and another one for animators was formed, and, in 1925, a faculty for cameramen.

Sergei Eisenstein devoted much time and attention to the VGIK. By 1928 he was head of the experimental workshop with Georgi and Sergei Vasiliev (who were later to shoot the Soviet classic *Chapayev*) among the pupils. Between 1932 and 1935 Eisenstein worked out a systematic course and the first programme of basic professional directors' teaching in the world. V. Pudovkin, A. Dovzhenko, I. Savchenko, N. Zarkhi, E. Tisse and Y. Zhelyabuzhsky, all taught there. In 1931, the cinemathèque of the VGIK was formed, housing 500 selected Soviet and foreign films. During the war, the VGIK was evacuated and set up temporarily at Alma-Ata (in Kazakhstan). Many students of the VGIK served as newsreel cameramen at the front, during the war.

After the war, the activity of the VGIK died down. Young people were not allowed to make films—only a handful of trusted comrades, the so-called Olympians, made a few. Even the Government newspaper *Izvestia* wrote (after Stalin's death, naturally): 'The period of few pictures is a barrier to youth.' Many young people had to change their careers because of the lack of any perspective. After Stalin's death young VGIK graduates came to the studios and some, V. Basov and M. Korchagin, for instance, were reluctantly given artistic tasks to fulfil. In 1955 three young VGIK graduates produced films: the Georgians T. Abuladze and R. Chkheidze made a screen version of the classical story *Lurdzha Magdany,* and S. Samsonov made *The Grasshopper* after Chekhov. *Lurdzha Magdany* was one of the films which started a new epoch in Soviet cinema. After the pseudo-historical pictures of Stalin's trusted Olympian, Chiaureli, a fresh and truthful picture reached the screens. The lecturers at VGIK, directors of the older generation— S. Gerassimov, G. Alexandrov, G. Roshal, L. Arnstam, S. Vasiliev, etc. did not take up contemporary subjects, and for years made no films at all, devoting themselves to teaching. In the years 1953–55 sixty-three young directors, thirty cameramen and thirty set-designers were given opportunities to make films.

The current director of the VGIK is Professor A. N. Groshev.

PART I   TOWARDS A NEW CINEMA

1 The Departure from Social Realism

At the beginning of the sixties, when a fresh breeze blew through the studios, the young film makers at once seized the opportunity to display their artistic individuality. One could now find a deep interest in contemporary society, and an analytical approach to the typical in everyday life. The main factor of this period, however, was a turning away from social realism. The young directors rejected conformist methods of film making, which had been *de rigueur* for film makers for over twenty-five years. This was not only apparent in films on modern subjects but especially in those on such themes as the Revolution and the Civil War—which were the worst affected by the rigid ideology. These canonised themes could not be ignored, even in the new conditions, but they were treated in a different way. In general, the result was films of great cruelty and violence, reflecting the harshness of that period.

One could discern not only a reappraisal of themes but also the influence of some modern non-Russian masters—Wajda in Mikhalkov-Konchalovsky's case, while Tarkovsky was affected by the visual aspect of French and Italian directors. When *The First Teacher* and *Ivan's Childhood* appeared in Russia, the official critics were dumbfounded and very unsure of their own reaction without clear-cut leads from above—ideologically the films were absolutely in order, but the whole treatment of the subjects was disconcertingly original. After lengthy deliberation it was officially decided to accept these films as new masterpieces of the Russian cinema.

Andrei Tarkovsky

Of the young directors, one man is undoubtedly the key figure: Andrei Tarkovsky. He, Mikhalkov-Konchalovsky and Vadim Yusov were at the VGIK together. In 1961, their diploma work, a short called *The Steam-roller and the Violin*, was completed. It is the touching story of a friendship between a frail boy violinist, named Sasha, and a robust driver of a steam-roller, Sergei. Before he meets Sergei, Sasha is like a hot-house plant, living in his little, comfortable, closed world. Sergei opens up a fresh and fascinating universe, which the sensitive young musician drinks in avidly; and he has optimistic dreams of his vocation as an artist. Yusov's camera contrives to recreate the world through a child's eyes by the masterly use of soft lights and by subtle gradations of atmosphere, which almost achieve the effect of a painting. *The Steam-roller and the Violin* won a prize at the New York festival.

The creative individuality of Tarkovsky, as an exponent of the new Soviet cinema, was fully realised in his first feature, *Ivan's Childhood* (1962). This is a harsh and tragic film about a ruined childhood, portrayed without a trace of sentimentality. Clever camera movements and editing make this visually very memorable. The sombre reality of the present is intercut with flashbacks. Yusov's camerawork was a revelation. With a painter's subtlety he identifies himself completely with the director's intentions. For instance, at one point in the film two patches of woodland – a forest of white birches and a wilderness of threatening black, burnt stumps – are framed together, not as two landscapes, but as two embodied visual symbols of life and death; and such visual devices are employed throughout the film, to great effect. Tarkovsky bases his whole approach on contrasts of war and childhood, war and nature, and reality and dreams, using symbolic shots.

Many Soviet directors have since followed his special methods. All Tarkovsky's works, and those influenced by him, are instantly recognisable by the complex 'lateral' build-up of associations, and the wealth of metaphorical and symbolic elements. In *Ivan's Childhood* one is literally haunted by the face of the boy—dark, emaciated, with nervous lips and tired, angry eyes, not like a child's face at all, more like the face of a brow-beaten old man. This impression is so vivid that one almost sees wrinkles on Ivan's face, though this is all in the imagination. Yusov's harsh lighting, from below, underlines the features even more, transforming the small boy into a symbolic figure like a Biblical martyr. *Ivan's Childhood*, a *tour de force*, won fifteen awards at international events, among them the Golden Lion in Venice and the Selznick prize in the USA.

Tarkovsky's second feature, *Andrei Rublev* (1966) is dealt with later, at length. This director is currently completing a third feature in colour, *Solaris*, from a novel by the Polish science-fiction writer, Stanislaw Lemm. *Solaris*, dealing with the exploration of space, may be the Soviet answer to Kubrick's *2001*. Cosmonauts find the embodiment of their dreams on a planet which they have been trying to reach for 200 years. Tarkovsky has invited about thirty foreign correspondents in Moscow to take part as scientists and journalists in one of the main episodes of the film. Among the players are the Lithuanian, Donatas Banionis, and Yuri Yarvet, and there is an acting appearance by the director of *Shadows of Our Forgotten Ancestors*, Sergei Paradzhanov, as well.

Andron Mikhalkov-Konchalovsky

Mikhalkov-Konchalovsky started directing with a short, *The Boy and the Pigeon* (1962) which he made with his friend E. Ostashenko, from his own script. This colour film, a lyrical miniature, won the Bronze Lion, the Grand Prix of the International Film Festival for Children in Venice. After that, Mikhalkov-Konchalovsky made *The First Teacher* (1965), adapted from a novel by the contemporary Kirghiz writer, Chingiz Aytmatov.

It deals with the establishment of Soviet rule in Kirghizia in 1923. The Civil War has only just ended. Duyshen, an ex-Red Army soldier, arrives in a small Kirghiz village and is appointed a teacher in the local school—which he has to build up himself. Although his own education leaves much to be desired, he firmly believes that only learning will help these ignorant people, ridden with age-old prejudices, to get a better deal. The villagers give Duyshen the cold shoulder, and are absolutely disinterested in building a school. So Duyshen, with his bare hands and, aided only by children, rebuilds a disused barn, persuades the parents to let the children go to school and even has to carry them himself, one by one, over the icy waters of mountain creeks. Often he gets too involved in his struggle, and acts like a fanatic, but he is always unshakably convinced of the rightness of his cause. A local rich man is attracted by one of Duyshen's pupils,

The Departure from Social Realism

The First Teacher by Andron Mikhalkov-Konchalovsky with Natalia Arinbasarova in the lead

a young girl called Altynay. The man's gang beat up Duyshen, when he tries to protect the girl, and they kidnap her. Duyshen approaches the authorities, then raids the enemy camp in the company of state security men, and rescues the raped girl. The whole village is now against Altynay, – who has broken the Muslim custom of the absolute obedience of woman – and against the teacher, who has also broken religious taboos, especially as he has done it with the help of outside forces, which are unpopular with the villagers. Duyshen is ordered from the village and he takes Altynay, with whom he has fallen in love, along with him. But his sense of revolutionary duty calls him back: the gang of the arrested rich man has taken revenge by burning down his 'school'. The fanatic Duyshen decides not to give up. He will build a new school. To this end he fells a solitary poplar, which has been the pride of the village for many, many years. The sound of the axe is the death-knell of a chapter of life, echoing the same episode in Chekhov's *Cherry Orchard*, but in a different tone and context.

The First Teacher is an adaptation of a literary work, but it is completely recreated for the screen by the director. The conflict is genuine, as are the people involved, and the treatment is personalised and far from a schematic and lifeless social realist good guys–bad guys travesty, even though subjects dealing with revolutionary events belong to a rigidly controlled category of art in Russia. The drama is treated, as a conflict in human terms. It is possible that Mikhalkov-Konchalovsky was to some extent influenced in his approach by Protazanov's *The Forty First* (1927), in which the canonised subjects of the Revolution and the Civil War are also shown through peoples' eyes, as they are caught in the iron grip of historical events. Indeed, *The First Teacher* can be regarded as the beginning of the 'independent cinema' (in the sense we are using this term).

The other new tendency of the young Soviet film makers is towards the romantic and the fantastic. Their films are a flight from drab reality, and they depict exotic places, eccentricities, unusual characters and the colourful past. This second trend has created a whole new school, in contrast to the 'kitchen sink' films of the Soviet neo-realists, which became quite common in the second half of the fifties.

Emergence of a New School
The new creative school in the Soviet cinema emerged spontaneously. It had neither a theoretical manifesto (as was the case with Eisenstein's 'Montage of attractions', the theories of Kuleshov, the FEX* group

* Factory of the eccentric actor.

of Kozintsev and Trauberg, LEF (Left Front of the Arts) and Dziga Vertov's declarations), nor a 'leader'. The pictures made by the new school are very different in character from each other. A true artist always reveals something new in his art, by following his own original ways, which are often considered 'wrong' at first. To understand this new direction in films, one has first of all to analyse some of them.

Mikhalkov-Konchalovsky followed *The First Teacher* with *A Nest of Gentlefolk* (1969), adapted from Turgenev's novel. Turgenev succeeded in conveying subtle aspects of the characters' psychological make-up, the peculiar charm of the Russian country-folk, and nature. In pain or doubt, grief or happiness, his characters (like the author himself, who was a keen hunter) turn to nature and find in it, as in a close friend, support and consolation. *A Nest of Gentlefolk* is based on one of the finest novels in Russian literature. The hero is Fyodor Lavretsky, the last of a long line of gentry, a representative of the Russian nobility of the mid-nineteenth century, a kind-hearted, liberal-minded, well educated and yet very impractical man. He is regarded as a misfit, as having no real place in the hierarchical society with a monarchy on the Prussian model. While realising the false pretensions, injustices and viciousness of his environment, he can offer nothing practical or active to counter it. Lavretsky is a complicated, contradictory character; he is strongly tied to the Russian soil and to his ancestors but gnawed by countless doubts and emotions. Hence his conflict with the world, his psychological drama. Everyone in the same milieu reflects this conflict: his wife, Varvara Petrovna, his beloved Liza, and Panshin, a man of rational and practical views. Each character in the film is impressive and highly individual. After a lengthy and thorough search, suitable actors were found—the part of Panshin was played by Victor Sergachev of the Moscow 'Sovremennik' Theatre; the Polish actress, Beata Tyszkiewicz, was Varvara Petrovna; Lavretzky was a gifted actor, Leonid Kulagin, from the Leningrad Bolshoi Drama Theatre; and Liza—Irina Kupchenko, a second-year student at the Shchukin Theatre School, in her first film role. As for the method of directing the actors, Mikhalkov-Konchalovsky said:

'Mainly improvisation. I believe this gives an actor the opportunity to show his professional skill and at the same time to reveal his most profound qualities.

A Nest of Gentlefolk by Andron Mikhalkov-Konchalovsky with Irina Kupchenko as Liza Kalitina

The Departure from Social Realism

Uncle Vanya by Andron Mikhalkov-Konchalovsky (Sergei Bondarchuk as Dr Astrov)

Improvisation, however, demands thorough and serious training. The modern world needs Turgenev, just as it needs Dostoyevsky and Tolstoy.'

The film version of *A Nest of Gentlefolk* concentrates on the yearnings of modern man after the romantic past, while the sociological and dramatic conflicts of the novel retreat into the background. Scores of similar films in contemporary Russia indicate that, despite difficulties, the film maker now has more scope for experiment and self-expression, and no longer has to suffer the suffocating control experienced earlier. Indeed, film making is the most free and alive of all the arts in Russia today.

After *A Nest of Gentlefolk*, Mikhalkov-Konchalovsky remained in the realm of Russian classical literature. He turned to Chekhov's *Uncle Vanya*. Astrov was played by S. Bondarchuk, Uncle Vanya by I. Smoktunovsky. *Uncle Vanya* aroused controversy during shooting, which did not subside after the appearance of the film. Mikhalkov-Konchalovsky has kept his quiet, unhurried style and low-key approach. His film versions of Russian classics are the only ones which retain the unmistakable flavour and craftsmanship of the original works.

On the Eve of Ivan Kupala Day by Yuri Ilyenko

Young Soviet Film Makers

The cameraman Yuri Ilyenko works in a colourful, fanciful style. He started as a director of photography after graduating from the VGIK in 1960, working at the Yalta Studio in the Crimea on *Goodbye, Doves* (1961) and *Somewhere There Is a Son* (1962). Then, at the Dovzhenko Studio in Kiev, he shot Paradzhanov's feature film *Shadows of Our Forgotten Ancestors* (1964), which won a prize for its brilliant camerawork at the Mar-del-Plata Festival, and more than a dozen other prizes for camerawork, lighting and colour at other festivals. Paradzhanov's film began a new trend in the Soviet cinema art, towards the *cinema of images*. The main characteristics of this school are a slight story, and concentration on folklore, ethnography, exotic motifs and, in general, the visual elements of the film. These films resemble a beautiful painting, an old print or a drawing, rather than the usual 'filmed play' so well known to the public, where a dramatic story is acted out on the screen.

After *Shadows of Our Forgotten Ancestors*, Ilyenko became a director-cameraman himself and made a comedy, *On the Eve of Ivan Kupala Day* (1968), from a story by Nikolai Gogol. He used even more dazzling images, based on the rich folklore of the Ukraine, which is extremely suitable for such treatment. The legend about the intrigues of the devil, who tries to buy the soul of a simple cossack for gold, becomes a phantasmagoria on Ukrainian motifs, with colourful displays of the eighteenth-century court of Catherine the Great and her favourite, Prince Potemkin; an invasion of the Crimean Tartars; and cossack frenzy at feasts and in battle. The last remnants of realism are abandoned as we enter a kingdom of metaphors and allegories, where the simple figures of folklore grow into symbols with elusive meaning, half comical, half menacing.

Other films of this school also deal with stories set in the past—Paradzhanov's *The Colour of the Pomegranate (Sayat Nova)*, and the Georgian film, *The Appeal*, by Abuladze and Kveselava. *The Appeal* is a staged version of poems by the nineteenth-century Georgian poet Vazha Pshavela. Its two episodes deal with the ancient custom of vendettas. The first story tells about a tribe chasing a man, from a different part of the country, on whom the curse of a blood-feud is placed, simply because one of his relatives was involved in a murder. In the second episode, a hunter lost in the mountains finds refuge in a strange village. However, again through no fault of his own, he is recognised to be under the bloody curse of the mountain-dwellers' vendetta, is tried by the whole village and condemned to death. This romantic, even cruel, film is outstanding because of the exact and inspired camerawork of the young A. Antipenko.

There have been attempts to treat contemporary subjects in this manner but they have failed. One example of this is the most recent film by Ilyenko, *White Bird with a Black Spot* (1971); but the ethnographical splendour does not enrich the ideological subject matter, which concerns the struggle between anti-Nazi and anti-communist partisans.

The new school was started by Mikhalkov-Konchalovsky (*A Nest of Gentlefolk*) and Paradzhanov (*Shadows of Our Forgotten Ancestors*), as a spontaneous reaction against social realism, and subsequently developed into a movement which consciously tries to avoid contemporary subjects and strives towards complete individuality. More and more young directors are joining this movement; a recent example is Leonid Osyka with his phenomenal *Zakhar Berkut* (1972), a historic pageant which can be compared with Tarkovsky's *Andrei Rublev*.

2 Controversial Directors

Tarkovsky's ANDREI RUBLEV

Many of the young directors are regarded as controversial, especially Andrei Tarkovsky. After *Ivan's Childhood* his search for new ways of self-expression culminated in *Andrei Rublev*, where he collaborated with the same team of Yusov and Mikhalkov-Konchalovsky. The film deals with fifteenth-century Russia and the life of the greatest of the Russian icon painters, Andrei Rublev. *Passion According To Andrei*, as it was originally called, consists of a string of loosely-connected episodes, encompassing the most prolific years in the painter-monk's life (1400–25). *Andrei Rublev* is a sombre film with traditional Russian religious undertones. The religious subject is treated here rather from an aesthetic point of view, but with a certain sympathy, which is a new approach for Soviet cinema. It is this aspect which caused trouble with the censors. It was only after a great struggle that the film was released in December 1971. *Andrei Rublev*, however, became widely known after the Cannes Festival in 1969.

Rublev was one of several legendary, almost mythical Russian painters, who lived long ago in the confusion of medieval times. Little is known of them save their names—even the dates of their births and deaths can only be guessed—but the work of their hands is still with us and has lost none of its stunning beauty and freshness.

It is a mystery how a man like Rublev could have

Director Andrei Tarkovsky

emerged in those dark times when the land was constantly rent by feudal clashes, ruined by the Tartar hordes, drained by bloodshed, hungry and impoverished. Rublev's call for brotherhood came when blood flowed in rivers and human life was not worth a snap of the fingers. It is known only that Rublev was born before the battle of Kulikovo (the beginning of Russia's liberation from Tartar rule, after several centuries of slavery), at the turn of the fourteenth and fifteenth centuries. Rublev worked as an icon-painter in Vladimir, Novgorod and Moscow; was a monk, studied under Daniil Chorny and was spiritually influenced by St Sergei Radonezhsky, a figure comparable in medieval Russia to St Francis of Assisi.

And this is all we know of his life. Naturally, no biographical film can be made from such sparse material. Tarkovsky has said:

'The main thing for us is the problem of the artist, the man standing amid a concentration of the struggles, the passions, the ideas of his epoch, and his interrelations with the people, the authorities, his colleagues. In *Rublev* we want to express the process of an artist's relationship with the world, to show how real emotional experience helps him to determine his attitude to the world and to himself. After breaking with the numb, canonical dogma, he, an innovator, finally comes to the recognition of living tradition. But he does not make a fetish of it, he accepts it only in so far as it becomes part of his creative life-experience. The meagreness of information about Rublev gives us a certain freedom. In the invented biography we have inserted our own conceptions, our ideas of art, we look at him from the twentieth century, from the standpoint of our own world-view. This is no artificially strained interpretation. Rublev's own work, so incredibly ahead of its time, makes it possible for us to reconstruct his ideas with imperishable values that link up with our own times. Rublev worked in the canonical manner, in the narrow frame of traditional icon-painting into which he did not introduce, like the early Italian artists of the Renaissance, any wordly elements. But within this framework he was able to progress far ahead of his time ideologically, to create ethical ideals for the people, ideals of harmony, brotherhood and unity. His whole urge was towards the future, and in this lies his genius. Unlike Theophanes the Greek, who propounded the idea of Judgement Day, who found in Man only the embodiment of sin and vice, and in God a vengeful, punitive being, Rublev placed Man first. In Man he sought God, he regarded him as the house in which God lived. In other words, Rublev was a man who reacted to everything around which other people would tend to find commonplaces. I do not understand purely historical films which have no relevance for the present. For me the most important thing is to use historical material to express Man's ideas and to create contemporary characters. It would be a pity if our film were judged from the scientific and historical point of view—such judgement could kill Shakespeare who, whether he wrote about the historical Caesar or the legendary Danish prince Hamlet, always remained true to the problems of his *own* time. As for the epoch, which was studied well, we try to be precise. Any exotic effects or stylisation are unacceptable. This applies to the language as well. People in the film use simple colloquial Russian without archaic expressions or modern terminology.'

The film consists of ten episodes, like pages from Rublev's life—the story of his inner development, his outlook, the formation of his striking, unbending character. His social surroundings also play a big part. Tarkovsky and Mikhalkov-Konchalovsky visited many places connected with Rublev's life and work and also consulted historians and art scholars. It is interesting to note that the film was shot on location in the ancient cities of Russia – Pskov, Novgorod, Vladimir – and on Lake Ladoga, in Izborsk, along the Pechora and the Nerl and in the Andronikov Monastery. The interiors and sets were designed by famous artists— Ippolit Novoderezhkin, Stepan Voronkov, Yevgeni Cherniaev and Yevgeni Korablyov. A very talented young composer, Vyacheslav Ovchinnikov, wrote the music. Since no iconographic material remains to show the appearance of Rublev and his associates, the choice of an actor for the rôle should not have presented any particular difficulties. There was complete freedom, and nobody could criticise the choice. Eventually Anatoli Solonitsyn from the Sverdlovsk Theatre was chosen. Tarkovsky said about the actor for the lead:

'We visualise Andrei Rublev as a man of great inner strength, quick and highly strung. But outwardly he is restrained and silent, a deep, profound thinker. Consequently the actor must be able to hold in leash a seething inner temperament. This is highly important, for there are many scenes in the script when Rublev's outward actions and movements do not conform to what is going on inside him. Any sickly sweet sentimentality would be quite inadmissible. The canonical representation of Rublev is a youthful angelic figure with enormous blue eyes; this is how Mikhail Nesterov* depicted him on canvas, and Ilya Glazunov* tried to follow suit. But he must have been far from all this, and the clarity of his work arises from something very different, from a harmonious cognition of the world. This clarity cost Rublev tremendous effort, it was born of agitation and disturbance.'

Another important hero of the film, the monk Kirill, is very interesting. He was similar to Rublev in temperament and force, with a profound and passionate nature, but his tragedy was that he was not gifted. It must be recalled that in those years the problem of the personality, the individuality of an artist (especially in the icon-painting tradition) did not arise: they were artisans in one shop. Kirill, like Salieri, did not realise his own malice and hatred, his envy and powerlessness, he simply suffered because his work did not come out as well as Rublev's. This complex character was splendidly acted by Ivan Lapikov.

The film is in black-and-white, and wide screen, but in the final part colour is used for the showing of Rublev's pictures. A procession with his famous Trinity icon† is shown in close-up. There is a rather ambiguous ending, with torrential rain threatening to wash away the colours of the icon: it is obviously symbolic, but can be explained in several ways. It is interesting to note that at the 1971 Belgrade Festival *Andrei Rublev* was cancelled by the Soviet authorities on the grounds that 'it does not correspond to historical truth . . . .'

---

* Russian painter (1862–1942) famous for historical and religious paintings.

* A fashionable painter in present-day Russia, much influenced by the icon tradition of painting.

† This painting occupies a central place in Russian art, comparable to Raphael's Sistine Madonna in Western Europe.

Young Soviet Film Makers

Mikhalkov-Konchalovsky's ASYA'S HAPPINESS

Immediately after *Andrei Rublev*, Mikhalkov-Konchalovsky started to shoot *Asya, the Lame* or *The Story of Asya Klyachkina, Who Fell in Love But Never Married* (1966). The young scriptwriter, Yuri Klepikov, had waited three years for the opportunity to make this film with Mikhalkov-Konchalovsky. It is a story of an ordinary contemporary village somewhere in Russia. Unlike *The Chairman* by A. Saltykov, it does not deal with difficult social problems, like the kolkhoz (collective farm) order.

Asya's Happiness (the final title of the film), is about personal experience, and is treated with typical Russian flair. The story is very simple: a young village girl, Asya, who is slightly lame, becomes pregnant by a village lad, whom she loves very much, but the boy is not really interested in her. In the end, she refuses a marriage proposal from a worker living in a city, which would have given her the opportunity to leave the miserable life in the village. She also refuses her former lover who comes, too late, to appreciate her personality. That is all. Despite the everyday story and ordinary setting, the film is unusual in many respects. It outgrows its conventional frame and takes in 'documentary' episodes of village life, whereas rural life in Soviet cinema is usually depicted unrealistically, heavily coloured by wishful thinking. This is not a documentary embellishment to a feature film, but is an intrusion of the cinema into real human life. Only three professional actors are in the film, which is in the tradition of Kinoglaz—made on location, with local people in their everyday dress. It gave such a true picture of the extremely hard life of the contemporary Soviet village that it was promptly 'shelved'.

Elem Klimov's BITTER SATIRES

It is interesting to note that the majority of young directors came into films from scientific professions. Elem Klimov is a former member of the technical intelligentsia, a graduate of an aviation institute, who later came to the VGIK. He soon became distinguished in his new profession—for a number of years no show of students' work from VGIK was complete without his hilarious silent short, *The Fiancée*. Klimov also acquired, while still at the VGIK, a reputation for satirical shorts, including *Careful—Banality!* and the documentary *Look, the Sky!* One could regard *Welcome* as a sequel to these.

In 1964, he submitted *Welcome* for his diploma work. A medium-length feature, it is a comedy for grown-ups, who were once children, and for children who will one day grow up. It is a biting satire on conditions in the Soviet Union, and made audiences cry with laughter. But primarily it is a determined attack on bureaucracy gone mad, on an order of things, where life is controlled and regimented almost out of existence, but on the most humane and noble pretexts.

The scriptwriters, Semyon Lungin and Ilya Nusinov, wrote the very witty script with its engaging story-line, and the director Klimov used all the possibilities of situation and dialogue to the full.

The opening shots of a whole avenue of horrid plaster statues of boys, for instance, allude to similar masterpieces of social realism, which one may still encounter in many Russian cities, towns and even villages. Above the gates is a huge poster proclaiming 'Welcome', but at the entrance we see a small sign 'No unauthorised entry'. The 'hero', Dynin, is director of a Young Pioneer (Communist boy-scouts) summer camp. He may be sincere and even good natured, but he is also narrow minded, afraid of everything new and a passionate transmitter of bureaucratic instructions. He puts up forbidding signs everywhere 'No trespassing', 'Do not touch', 'Do not play in the river', etc. In fact, nearly everything in the camp is forbidden and restricted: escape is impossible. The children bathe in a lake – literally enclosed in a net – but Kostya Inochkin, the independent-minded hero of the comedy, makes a hole in the net and escapes to an island. For this he is expelled from the camp.

On the way home, he imagines what will be his due after such disgrace: his grandmother (who, by the way, looks exactly like Khruschev), dies instantly of a broken heart; a huge funeral procession, taking the shape of a menacing question mark, carries banners – 'Why did you kill your grandmother?' – and a white-bearded old man cries in an impassioned speech that he never made any trouble for his grandmother, how could Kostya dare to do this horrible thing? Kostya decides that he cannot possibly face this and returns secretly to the camp to lead an 'underground' life. The story of the film is made up of a comical war between the children, who hide Kostya, and the superbly parodied 'establishment', trying to catch him. Later on he is the winner of the camp's traditional carnival, despite the intrigues of the director, who had connected some hopes of personal advancement with the event.

The allegory was too transparent not to be noticed by the censors and the film was not passed for general release during Khrushchev's time, but was shown in some clubs a few years later. Many admire Klimov greatly, some bitterly resent his work. His second feature, *The Adventures of a Dentist* (1967) was scripted by a well-known playwright Alexander Volodin, who later became a director himself. Here the difficulties began with the script, which was

Adventures of a Dentist
by Elem Klimov

officially unacceptable. The subject of this controversial film is the obligation of Soviet society towards a talented man. After a long struggle the script was finally 'pushed through'. The film tells about a young dentist, who comes to a town after graduating from a medical school. He starts work in a hospital and, owing to his talent, soon becomes very popular. Other people in the hospital envy him, and intrigues multiply. This brilliant comedy further substantiates Klimov's reputation as a sharp satirist. After *The Adventures of a Dentist* the director turned to the commercial cinema.

Larissa Shepitko
Larissa Shepitko is one of the very few young women among controversial film makers at present. She came to Moscow from the Ukraine to study at the Cinema Institute, and became a pupil of Dovzhenko. Her first short, *Living Water* (1960) carries the mark of her teacher. Shepitko is fascinated by painting and music, and her films bear witness of this. Her diploma work *Heat* (1963), was made in the Kirghizian steppes. She was fortunate in having a very good script by S. Lungin and I. Nusinov, and an excellent cameraman, Yuri Sokol (all friends from VGIK times). The lead was taken by a Kirghizian student of the director's department of VGIK, Bolot Shamshiev, who was later to become a director himself.

Heat was made under gruelling conditions, on barren steppes without a single tree for shade, under the burning sun, when the temperature rose to 40–50°C, and film stock literally melted in the heat. On top of all this the 22-year-old girl-director fell ill in the middle of the shooting. But she did not give up and had herself transported to location every day on a stretcher. It is a cruel film about hard work and human conflicts in the arid semi-desert of Central Asia, without the usual propagandist highflown phrases of the official press and newsreels.

Shepitko made her second feature, *Wings*, in 1966, which deals with the problem of the generation gap. The heroine, Nadezhda Petrovna, was a much decorated fighter pilot during the war who shot down many German aircraft. She recalls the years of her militant youth, and her friends who did not return. She secretly envies those who are still serving in aviation, because she herself cannot work as a pilot any more. She is now forty-two, a deputy of the Town Soviet (Council), respected and honoured by the local people, but her personal life is less happy. She is lonely and does not like her job as director of a vocational school. The pupils do not like her either—her way of ordering people around, her indifference, her heartless manner. A pupil of her school, looking directly into her face, says, 'I detest you!' Even her

On location of *Heat* by Larissa Shepitko

Controversial Directors

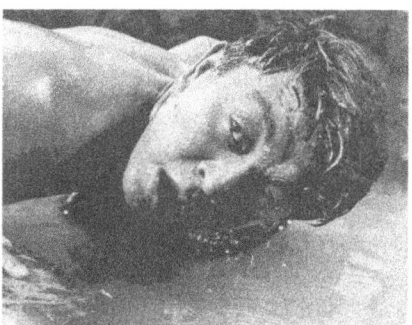

Heat by Larissa Shepitko

only daughter has no common language with her. Nadezhda Petrovna, of course, tries to understand, but her puritanism (the daughter has a lover) prevents it. *Wings* is built around one actress, Maya Bulgakova, as Nadezhda Petrovna, who had previously appeared only in small rôles, without much hope of a breakthrough. Such a film naturally aroused a violent controversy in the Press: 'We have no conflicts between parents and children', 'To show a war veteran in this way is to jeer at the war heroes', and so on.

Now Shepitko is making a film about modern youth *You and I*, at Norilsk, in deepest Siberia, which in Stalin's time was the capital of a huge region populated almost exclusively by concentration camp inmates. The famous poetess, Bella Akhmadulina, a former wife of Yevgeni Yevtushenko, will act in the film.

Wings by Larissa Shepitko

Western Influence

Simultaneously with the appearance of working-class life on the screen in British cinema (*Saturday Night and Sunday Morning*, 1960; *A Taste of Honey*, 1962;

Young Soviet Film Makers

Director Larissa Shepitko on location of her new film *You and I*

The Loneliness of the Long Distance Runner, 1962; *This Sporting Life*, 1963), the same subject emerged in Soviet films. Many will remember the scandal over *I Am Twenty*, by the Georgian director Marlen Khutsiev, when Khrushchev personally became involved. It was still a revelation, despite being severely cut, when it appeared in 1961. The film has been remade many times. A second film on this subject came out in 1965, *Our House*, by director Vassili Pronin and the controversial young scriptwriter Yevgeni Grigoriev. Both films caused sharp controversy—admiration on one side and total rejection on the other.

In 1968, a VGIK graduate, Mark Osepyan, made his first feature film *Three Days of Victor Chernyshev*, scripted by the same writer, Yevgeni Grigoriev. Complete dissociation from social realism had taken place. Mikhail Papava, a critic and scriptwriter of the older generation (one of the scriptwriters of *Ivan's Childhood*) said about *Three Days:* '... for a long time we were in the shadow of the dubious theory that you have to show life not as it really is, but as it should be.' Now young film makers like Mark Osepyan and Yevgeni Grigoriev, liberated from the fetters of social realism, were able to make a very vivid film about the lives of working-class youth. *Three Days* ... is very similar to Karel Reisz's *Saturday Night and Sunday Morning*. When the film was released, some of the conformist critics demagogically tried to present it as a slur on the unblemished reputation of the working class ('How can one show a young worker as a layabout and hooligan!')

Alexei Saltykov

Alexei Saltykov became famous after his feature *The Chairman* (1964). Prior to this he had made the marvellous children's comedy *My Friend, Kolka*, with Alexander Mitta. *The Chairman*, scripted by the well-known writer, Yuri Nagibin, is a film about the extremely touchy subject of present-day rural life— the difficult situation in the kolkhozes (collective farms), which nobody has dared or would have been allowed to discuss earlier. The film exploded like a bomb on the Soviet press and public, because it dared to tell the truth for the first time. The editorial offices of papers and magazines were flooded with letters, and at booking-offices endless queues formed for tickets. The story concerns two brothers, one of whom is the chairman of a kolkhoz. He tries to compel everybody, including his brother, to work on the kolkhoz, and the film is simply the background to this.

After *The Chairman*, Saltykov started *The Director*, working from Yuri Nagibin's script, but in the middle of the shooting, the leading actor, the immensely popular Yevgeni Urbansky, was killed in a car crash on location, and the project was temporarily abandoned.

Saltykov's second feature was *The Kingdom of Women* (1967), also with Y. Nagibin. It is no less controversial than his first. The film tells of events taking place in a village during the German occupation. As is well known, there were scarcely any men left in the villages during the war: it *was* a veritable kingdom of women. *The Kingdom of Women* is a tragic, realistic, bloody story of the destinies of such a group of women. It was a great commercial success, but the critics were divided as to its merits.

After this, Saltykov finished *The Director* (1969). It deals truthfully with the Revolution, the Civil War, and the periods of industrialisation and collectivisation. Yuri Nagibin's script is based on the biography of Likhachev, the director of a well-known Moscow automobile works, which now, after his death, bears his name.

3 Young Intellectuals

In modern Russian cinema six directors stand out. Their films are marked by their individuality, vivid talent and romanticism. They are—Mikhail Bogin, Pavel Lubimov, Alexander Mitta, Vladimir Fetin, Vassili Shukshin and Gleb Panfilov. Only two of them, Lubimov and Fetin, came into films straight from school; the careers of the others evolved in a more complicated manner. Bogin studied for about two years at the Leningrad Polytechnical Institute; Shukshin had many different professions; Panfilov was a chemical engineer; and Mitta was a cartoonist on the satirical magazine *Krokodil* (the Soviet equivalent of *Punch*). All of them are more or less of the same age, but each has a clearly recognisable style which interprets his own special interests. All, with the exception of Panfilov and Shukshin (who started as an actor), began with successful shorts.

Mikhail Bogin

Mikhail Bogin's debut was the charming featurette *The Two* (1965), made at the Riga Film Studio in Latvia. It was unanimously approved by many cinéastes. *The Two* (written in collaboration with Y. Chulukin) is based on the love story of a young musician and a deaf-mute girl who lost her hearing in childhood, during the siege of Leningrad. Bogin has said:

'I wanted to make a film about human dignity, about the ability to overcome the dramatic turns of life. The desire grew stronger after I came to know Svetlana, a deaf-mute girl who became the prototype of the heroine of the film. Svetlana surprised me by her cheerfulness and by her wholesome attitude to life. Svetlana's fellow-sufferers, whom I got to know at the Expression and Gesture Theatre, also proved to be exceptionally lively, optimistic and interesting people.'

Sergei, a student at the Conservatoire, has spotted a girl in the street. He tries to start talking to her, but she walks on in silence and enters the building of a circus school. Sergei recalls that she has frequently ignored him in the past. He watches her and her friend's gesture language, and it dawns on him that she is deaf and dumb. Using a piece of paper and a pencil, while sitting on a boulevard bench, they get better acquainted with each other. He invites the girl, Natasha, to a concert she cannot hear. Her eyes follow the movements of the noiseless bows and rest on Sergei's inspired face—he is playing a solo on the oboe. And suddenly she recalls sounds she heard in her childhood. Sergei is played with great natural feeling by Valentin Smirnitsky, then a student at the Shchukin Theatre School, Natasha by Victoria Fyodorova, a young actress, whose other films include *Music*

Young Intellectuals

The Two by Mikhail Bogin with Valentin Smirnitsky as a young musician

Returned and *Good-bye, Boyhood!*

The Two is a lyrical short about love and loneliness. Bogin uses a hidden camera, shoots only on location or with real interiors and, is on principle, against studios. Not surprisingly his cameramen are newsreel reporters.

Bogin, a pupil of Joseph Heifitz, and assistant to him during work on *The Lady With a Little Dog*, is perhaps influenced by the romantic style of his master. When he was a student, Bogin made *Ten Seconds an Hour*—a highly original short, also shot with a hidden camera. It told of the tremendous work and thoughts of the artist, of the spiritual and physical tensions which lie behind a single instant of film.

His next film was the feature *Zosya* (1967), another romantic story, whose script was based on V. Bogomolov's short story *Zosya*, and a real-life incident during the war. In summer 1944, the remains of a Soviet army battalion retreated to a Polish village, Nowy Dwor, to rest. But instead of the promised two months rest, the soldiers stayed less than three days because the offensive started again. In these few days the young Russian officer Mikhail Kuzmin and

Young Soviet Film Makers

the Polish girl Zosya fell in love, but they did not even have time to tell each other about it—the war brought them together and tore them apart.

This Polish-Soviet co-production was filmed not far from Vilnius (Lithuania). Jerzy Lipman (*A Generation, The Shadow, Kanal, Lotna, Knife in the Water, Ashes,* etc.) was on camera; the set-designers were Roman Wolyniec and Leonard Mokicz; and the Polish actress Pola Raksa took the lead. *Zosya* by Michail Bogin is a very subtle and highly intellectual study of love and the cruelty of war.

Pavel Lubimov

Pavel Lubimov entered the VGIK in 1956, in Grigory Roshal's class. After his student film *The Gunshot*, he worked as an assistant director with S. Rostotsky on *In the Seven Winds* at the Gorky Film Studios in Moscow. He also acted in *Girls' Spring* and *End of the World*. Lubimov's first important work was his short *The Aunt With Violets* (1963), which won the Gold

The Women by Pavel Lubimov

Young Intellectuals

Hurrying On the Waves by Pavel Lubimov

Wawel Dragon at the Cracow Festival of documentary and short films. *The Aunt With Violets* tells the story of a Russian woman who saved the life of a baby during the war and, twenty-five years later, growing old, and dressed in a funny tasteless bonnet with violets, 'recognised' her Volodechka—a grown-up young man. The ridiculous, touching aunt with violets finds happiness again. *The Aunt With Violets* was half of a two-part film album, *The Youth;* the other half was the film of another Georgian director, Pavel Arsenov's *Sunflower*.

Lubimov's next film *The Women* (1966), was about women's psychology and their private life, their everyday joys, sorrows and their difficult lot. Three women are working at a furniture factory. Alka, young and naïve, is not happy—her boy-friend deceived and left her, so she had to leave her child with her mother in the country, and came to work at the factory. Yekaterina Bednova, a Communist activist at the factory, has helped many people, but when her only son, Zhenya, falls in love with Alka, who has an illegitimate child, she cannot muster enough courage to accept this. The third character is Duska, who dreams of marrying and raising a family, but all her lovers keep leaving her. The film was a great box-office success, because it dealt with the problems common to women everywhere. Lubimov turned out to be a brilliant psychologist.

After *The Women* he made an adaptation of the romantic novel by Alexander Grin, *Hurrying on the Waves* (1967), collaborating with Bulgarian film makers. *Hurrying on the Waves* is a fairy-tale about a

45

young man finding himself in an imaginary country, where he meets and falls in love with a young woman. Lubimov made the film harsher and more tragic than the literary original, in order to contrast the dreamer and the philistine, the romantic legend and grey everyday reality. Its success did much to consolidate Lubimov's reputation as a director.

In 1969 Lubimov made *A Day Ahead*, about the possessive love of a stepmother for her adopted child, a cynical and revolting youngster. *A Day Ahead* is another dramatic study of the female mind.

Alexander Mitta

After graduating from the VGIK, Alexander Mitta, a former cartoonist, co-directed (with A. Saltykov) the children's feature *My Friend Kolka* (1961) which had a screenplay by Alexander Khmelik and Sergei Yermolinsky. The film deals cheerfully with friendships between school-teachers and their pupils.

Mitta's next film was *Open the Door When the Bell Rings* (1966), with a script by the famous Soviet playwright, Alexander Volodin. A 12-year-old girl falls in love with an older pupil at her school, and follows him like a shadow. But when she sees him at the skating rink with another beautiful fair-haired girl, she feels pangs of jealousy, and is bitterly disappointed in her idol. The director had great difficulties in finding the right girl for this role. An advertisement to find the right girl was answered by 15,000 girls (and boys), who all arrived at the advertised place. All the streets and squares around the studio were crowded. One very old woman even tried to convince the director to take her grandson and said that she would gladly pay for it. Another woman from the provinces told the director that she would like to launch her two children on a cinema career, because she had no husband. One of the girls cried so bitterly, that Mitta took down her address. Somebody in the crowd shouted that the bespectacled man is taking down everybody who cries. A whole crowd of girls, laughing and trying to cry, fell upon the director. Helena Proklova, who eventually played the part, conveys excellently the quick lively reactions of the girl, without a trace of sentimentality.

In 1970 Mitta made his new film *Shine, O Shine My Star* (*The Comedy About Iskremas*). The film is about a pioneer of revolutionary art—an actor committed to the idea of people's theatre. He even takes a special

Open the Door When the Bell Rings by Alexander Mitta

Young Intellectuals

The New Girl by Pavel Lubimov

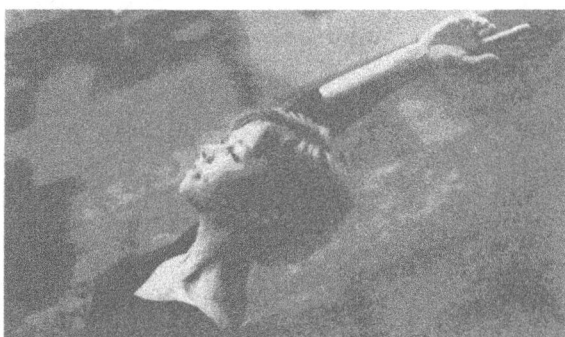

stage-name, Iskremas, which is an abbreviation of the words 'Revolutionary Art to the Masses'. With his vagrant group of players he visits different towns in Russia, which have been rent apart by the cruelties of the Civil War. He comes to a tragic end during a clash between hostile forces, but he leaves his pupils to continue his work. It is interesting to note that three controversial directors took part in the film as actors—Oleg Yefremov, chief director of the best Youth Theatre in Moscow, 'Sovremennik', Vladimir Naumov, and Marlen Khutsiev. Helena Proklova (eight years after *Open the Door When the Bell Rings*, and now a graduate of the VGIK), played the lead and Yuri Sokol was the principal cameraman.

Vladimir Fetin

Grigori Kozintsev's pupil, Vladimir Fetin, started his career with the beautiful short *The Foal* (1959). At that time he was much impressed by Albert Lamorisse and the film was made in the style of *Crin Blanc*.

In 1964 Fetin filmed *The Don Story*, which tells about human and inhuman relationships during the Civil War. A young woman, rescued by a Red cossack unit, falls in love with one of the Red Cavalry men. But at a crucial point she betrays the unit to its enemies (most cossacks were 'White' during the Civil War) and is shot by her lover—just when their son is being born. This bloody story was based on factual incidents of that horrible period.

After *The Don Story*, Fetin again screened a tragedy, *Virineya* (1969), adapted from a classic Soviet novel by Lidia Seifullina. A life or death struggle between Reds and Whites rages during the First World War and the Civil War in a Russian village. A young and beautiful peasant woman has met and fallen in love with a Bolshevik, whom she soon

47

intends to marry. But during a battle between the White cossacks and Red soldiers she is tragically killed. *Virineya* has a cameo rôle for the principal actress, Ludmila Chursina, who creates an image of tremendous dramatic tension, epitomised in the last scene of the film, when the dead Virineya is sitting, as if she were alive, in the same position as when she was shot—with horror-stricken cossacks running away from her.

Seifullina's novel was a great success in 1924, when it was first published. Two years later it was staged by the Vakhtangov Theatre, but in another few years the political situation had changed completely, the book was prohibited, the play taken off the stage, and Seifullina's husband, the journalist V. Pravdukhin, became a victim of the purges. Seifullina had to endure the humiliation of the public renunciation of her own book. However, the book has recently been reprinted, the play restaged, even an opera made on the subject, and finally a screen version of the story as well.

Gleb Panfilov

Gleb Panfilov is a newcomer. His brilliant debut *No Ford in the Fire* (1968), won the Grand Prix at the Locarno Festival in 1969. The film was made at

No Ford In the Fire by Gleb Panfilov with Inna Churikova and Mikhail Kononov

Young Intellectuals

The Debut by Gleb Panfilov (Inna Churikova in the lead)

Lenfilm Studio, by Panfilov, a former chemical engineer, and a very experienced playwright, Yevgeni Gabrilovich. The female lead, a gifted young girl (a painter in the primitivist manner, at the time of the Russian Civil War), was acted extremely naturally by Inna Churikova: her success was acknowledged by the jury at the Festival. Churikova is very much like a Soviet Giulietta Masina, with her touching and comic facial expressions, and awkward movements. Panfilov again entrusted Churikova with the lead in his second film *The Debut (A Girl from the Factory)* in 1970. The story depicts an unsophisticated, funny girl from a small town somewhere in Russia, who accidentally comes to play Joan of Arc in a film: thus Panfilov further developed his theme about ordinary people who unexpectedly turn out to be very gifted artists (the destiny of a painter in the first film, of an actress in the second). *The Debut*, moreover, has an interesting structure because there are really two intercut films — one about the everyday life of the factory girl, and another about her life in the film as Joan of Arc. *Debut* was a great success during the 1970 Soviet Film Week in Paris.

Vassili Shukshin
Vassili Shukshin has been much discussed in Russia, because he has achieved a remarkable and unusual combination as an actor/writer/director. His career began in acting with *Two Fyodors* by Khutsiev, *We, Two Men* (script by Anatoli Kuznetsov), *Alyonka* and others. His short stories are printed in the best Soviet literary magazine, *Novy Mir*.

As a director he has made a comedy, *There Was a Lad* (1964), about the gay adventures of a young, simple and kind-hearted truck driver, who comes across many new people and cannot remain cool and indifferent to anybody who needs help. At first the hero faces no problems; even the word 'problem' itself sounds strange to him, but gradually his naïve approach to life changes. This marvellous comedy won the Grand Prix at the Festival of Children's Films in Venice.

Two years later, Shukshin directed another feature *Your Son and Brother*, about the family of Yermolay Voyevodin, a Siberian peasant with four sons and one daughter. He lives in his old hut with his wife, daughter and youngest son Vassili. His son Stepan is in prison, because he has taken part in a drunken brawl, while Maxim and Ignat live in the town and do not want to have anything to do with the village. The old man understands Stepan, who, three months prior to his discharge from jail, escapes only in order to see his village, to sit at the table with his parents and fellow-villagers. He may be taken back to prison that very night, but he has acted the way his heart told him. Yermolay is more worried about his sons in the town. He dislikes the bragging of Ignat, a professional wrestler, who has been to many countries, and won many gold medals. The old man talks his youngest son, Vassili, into having a bout with Ignat, the town-dweller, and teach him that only village inhabitants are strong in mind and body. Neither does Yermolay understand Maxim, a building worker, who stays at a hostel, rejecting philistine comfort. The film is gently humorous and paints a true-to-life picture of the Siberian village of today.

It is also somewhat autobiographical, because Shukshin himself was born in Siberia and grew up in a similar village. He has changed professions many times—he was a fitter for quite a long time, then served in the Navy, was director of an evening school, then became a writer. Finally he graduated from the VGIK (M. Romm's class) as a director. In both his films he manages to create a world of his own, where nature is beautiful and severe, people are kind and artless; a world with the smells of earth, grass and resin, fuel and sweat.

In 1970, during the Soviet Film Week in Paris, Shukshin made a deep impression on the assembled company with his third film *Strange People*. The whole film, made after Shukshin's own short stories – 'Strange People', 'A Thousand Pardons, Ma'am' and 'Thoughts' – consists of three parts *Brother, The Tragic Shot* and *Thoughts*. The story of the first novel is very simple: a strange man travels to Yalta to see his brother (hence the title). This brother tries to marry him off: the aim is to find a woman with the right 'shop sign' (slang for face) and her own flat. The second novel, *The Tragic Shot*, is the best. It tells the story of an inveterate liar, Bronka Pupkov (everybody calls him by the diminutive Bronka, although he is already over fifty), who assures everybody that during the war he was personally entrusted with a mission to kill Hitler, but missed. The third novel – *Thoughts* – shows strange people in a fantastic village, where the farmers are much too intellectual for the present day. One can regard the story as the tale of some future village, where an ordinary man tries to think how he spent his life. This feature is an excellent example of *cinéma d'auteur*. Shukshin's film is very different from all previous films about rural life. It is intellectual, with many allegories and interesting shooting angles.

4 Comedies

The Twenties

The first significant director of comedies in Russia was Yakov Protazanov. His comedy on a foreign subject – *The Three Million Case* (1926) – is the best known. Being a great connoisseur of stage art, Protazanov discovered a large group of excellent comics, including Anatoli Ktorov, Maria Blumental-Tamarina, Mikhail Zharov and Igor Ilyinsky. It is worth noting that after the revolution Protazanov became an emigré, only to return three years later, in 1923, to continue making films. Two of his other well-known comedies, *The Tailor From Torzhok* (1925) and *Don Diego and Pelageia* (1928) are satires on bureaucracy and inhuman behaviour, indicating that at that time it was still possible to attack the *status quo*. Both comedies are bitterly satirical, with portraits of philistines, the emerging Soviet bureaucrats, scandal-mongers and similar pests of the society.

Other satirical film makers included such masters as Boris Barnet and Alexei Popov. The former made a lyrical comedy, *The Girl With the Hat-box* (1927) about the NEP (New Economic Policy), the latter a comedy, *Two Friends, a Model and a Girl-friend* (1928), about bureaucrats who have barricaded themselves behind all kinds of instructions, orders and various other papers. These were silent comedies about everyday life; but in the comedies of the twenties one can also discern elements of the eccentric and the slapstick.

In the 'funnies', the comical element was presented in the rather primitive form of slapstick jokes, chasing, breaking of plates and dishes, fights—almost a Hal Roach-Keystone cops approach. To increase the humour, the most absurd of basic life situations were freely used—people who were too thin or too fat, badly dressed, absent-minded, etc.

The late twenties was a most productive period, when B. Barnet, S. Komarov, A. Dmitriev and N. Stykovsky worked in films as varied as *Miss Mend* (1926), *The Kiss of Mary Pickford* (1927), *The Holiday of St Jorgen* (1930) and *The Three Million Case* (1926).

Other popular genres were the adventure comedy and the screened operetta. The most outstanding film of this kind was *The Little Red Devils* (1923), directed by Ivan Perestiani, about the hilarious adventures of boys serving as scouts in the Red cavalry. In this film exaggeration was indulged in, and the heroic deeds of the youngsters were performed by circus-players. Eccentric elements were also widely used in L. Kuleshov's experimental adventure film, *The Extraordinary Adventures of Mr West in the Land of the Bolsheviks* (1924).

The Thirties

In the thirties Soviet comedy went through a hard time: satire disappeared almost entirely. In 1932 the

Young Soviet Film Makers

RAPP (Russian Association of Proletarian Writers) was disbanded by a special Government decree. Comedies became more and more political, directed against foreign and internal 'enemies'. During the thirties, Alexander Medvedkin made his experimental short comedies *About Love* (1932) and *Happiness* (1934) on topical subjects. They were complicated in form and unsuitable for an unsophisticated public, but they look marvellous today.

As a contrast to this, the thirties saw the flourishing of the so-called 'new comedy', which was in effect a hymn of praise to the 'socialist reality' of the Stalin period. The main exponents of this 'new comedy' were Ivan Pyriev and Grigori Alexandrov. At the same time, a very interesting director, Alexander Ivanovsky, who had started before the Revolution, was still active. He shot such well-known comedies as *Musical Story* (1940) and *Anton Ivanovich is Angry* (1941). Pyriev made the notorious films *The Rich Bride* (1937), *The Tractor Drivers* (1939) and *The Swineherd and the Shepherd* (1941), all about 'happy kolkhoz life'. The

Anton Ivanovich is Angry with Ludmila Tselikovskaya in the lead

Anton Ivanovich is Angry (1941) by Alexander Ivanovsky

titles speak for themselves. Only after 1956, and Khrushchev's famous secret speech on Stalin, did it become possible to mete out nemesis on these ghastly and laboured propagandist exercises.

Grigori Alexandrov, a former assistant of Eisenstein's, made musicals—so-called revue comedies. His first comedy in this style, *The Jolly Fellows* (1934), was very successful, and starred the famous singer and jazz band leader, Leonid Utyosov. Another of his comedies, *The Circus* (1936), was a typical 'ideological' comedy, despite interesting circus and musical acts, and an idol of the public, Lubov Orlova, as an American circus star who is persecuted in America, because of her black child, and emigrates to the Soviet Union. Alexandrov later made *Volga, Volga* (1938) and *The Light Way* (1940), a variety dress revue.

Thirties comedy depended for its impact mainly upon acting. So-called 'positive heroes' reigned supreme—workers, who achieved records on the production line, and women who exceeded their work-quota at the workbench or in the kolkhoz fields.

Jolly Fellows is, nevertheless, a merry and highly

Anton Ivanovich is Angry

original theatrical film version of a jazz show conducted by Leonid Utyosov. The 'twelve musical numbers' that constitute the episodes of the film are linked by the story of a country girl who becomes an actress. The reason for the film's viability is its sunny optimism from beginning to end, an optimism that finds expression in youthful exuberance, vitality and naturalness. There is satire in it too—sharp barbs to needle petty-minded, malicious and ignorant hypocrites. The picture was made with superb professional skill: Dunayevsky's music, for instance, was a very important part of the first Soviet musical comedy. The film was a great success not only at home but abroad, particularly in France and Germany.

Since the War

Comedies were also popular during the war, especially *The New Adventures of Shveik* by S. Yutkevich. Instead of full-length films, specially prepared so-called 'fighting anthologies' were released, where information and propaganda strips were lightened by satirical and comic subjects.

After the war, comedy went through a crisis, because the slightest and most innocent satirical motives at once became suspect. Little wonder that people writing comedies were suffocating, and their numbers dwindling. Alexandrov made a very weak comedy, *The Spring* (1947), which was too long and very dull. Pyriev made two more of his kolkhoz films – *The Saga of the Siberian Land* (1947) and *The Kuban Cossacks* (1949) – almost perfect examples of the lying conformism of the period.

After Stalin's Death

The first comparatively well-known comedy after Stalin's death was *True Friends* (1954), by Mikhail Kalatozov. This film was liked by the public and the

Young Soviet Film Makers

Advertisement for *Kuban Cossacks* (director Ivan Pyriev)

critics for its human approach and truthfulness. Another successful satire of this period was *The Carnival Night* (1956) by the young director, Eldar Ryazanov; and Igor Ilyinsky made a comeback after almost twenty years absence from the screen! In these years, too, new talents emerged: Yuri Chulukin made the film *The Girls* (1962) about young people living in the Siberian taiga; and Leonid Gaydai made a screen adaptation of O. Henry's novel *Businessmen* (1963).

In the sixties, major young comedy film makers were Georgi Danelia, Gleb Panfilov, Elem Klimov, Alexander Mitta and Vassili Shukshin. Comical subjects, episodes and situations of all kinds appear in modern films. So, *I Walk About Moscow* (1964) by Georgi Danelia, could be called a realistic comedy; his recent film, *Cheer Up!* (1969) a tragi-comedy of the classical type.

I Walk About Moscow, with a controversial script by Gennadi Shpalikov, tells how a young writer comes to Moscow from Siberia for just one day and befriends a young worker and his group, who experience a number of funny and sad episodes. A veritable gallery of cameo parts, ingenious camerawork, shot in Moscow by Vadim Yusov, and an original score by the young composer Andrei Petrov, all create an atmosphere, where different shades of humour merge in a lyrical background.

Even more interesting, perhaps, is the latest film by Danelia. *Cheer Up!* is based on the novel *Mon Oncle Benjamin* by Claude Tillier; the film was scripted by Rezo Gabriadze and shot by Yusov. The action is transposed to pre-revolutionary Georgia, and the film suffused with Georgian spirit and colour. The young doctor Benjamin, with his many relatives, and friends, is happy but also has many worries—salaries are too meagre for a living, and the family is overburdened with children, and saved only by the fantastic efforts

Comedies

Cheer Up! by Georgi Danelia [4 slides]

of Benjamin's sister. The appearance of 'respectable poverty' is compared to the arrogance of the rich and powerful, who are always eager to demonstrate their superiority over ordinary human beings. In a gay atmosphere of drinking and singing folk-songs the narrative line develops—Benjamin's love for the young and naïve Mary, who in the end prefers a rather silly officer to Benjamin, and elopes with him from her parents' house. The film ends with simple-hearted Benjamin bringing Mary's child into the house of his sister, for Mary herself has been the victim of an accident. *Cheer Up!* then, is the first successful experiment in modern Soviet tragicomedy.

A few years ago *Beware, The Car!* (1966) by Eldar Ryazanov, was a great success. Innokenti Smoktunovsky played the leading role of a car thief, Detochkin. (The authors gave the name Detochkin – from the Russian word 'child' – to the hero on purpose.) This thief with a naïve character but a pure soul starts a struggle against injustice, not noticing the contradictions he falls into.

Among the so-called lyrical comedies of recent times one film is popular—*Three Plus Two* (1963) by Oganesyan. The subject is rather simple—two girlfriends, an actress and an animal trainer, go to the Crimea on vacation. It transpires that their favourite spot has already been occupied by a group of boys—a physics graduate, a veterinary surgeon and a future diplomat who categorically refuse to leave. Both 'enemy' camps settle side by side and are forced by circumstances to enter into 'diplomatic relations'. The

55

film was extremely successful, because of its uninhibited approach towards the problems of sophisticated modern young people.

The renaissance of the eccentric comedy owes most to the short films of Leonid Gaydai. The shorts, *The Dog Barboss and the Unusual Cross* and *The Alcoholmakers* (1961) were a revival of an almost forgotten genre. The films had a dynamic rhythm because of the quick cutting and rhythmic music and sound tracks: their whole structure and approach was very modern. In these and other films by Gayday, the comic actor, Yuri Nikulin, was a real revelation. This former circus performer reminds one instantly of the young Charlie Chaplin.

Three eccentric types of rogue – a fool, a coward and a man who has seen everything before – are generally included in all Gayday's films. They wander into Gayday's other film, *Operation 'Y' and Other Adventures of Shurik* (1965). In a comparatively short period Gayday made eight shorts and one full-length feature *The Captive Girl of the Caucasus or New Adventures of Shurik* (1967). The basis of this fantastic film is a quite realistic social phenomenon – the old Caucasian custom of stealing the bride before the wedding, but this custom is much adorned by improbable details, and the same three types of rogues appear again.

Among the eccentric comedies one has to place the shorts of the Georgian director, Mikhail Kobakhidze. In *The Wedding* (1964) the hero, a young pharmacist, falls in love with a girl whom he meets on a bus. Some time later, having made up his mind, he goes to her house to offer his hand and heart . . . but on the stairs he encounters a gay wedding procession: his beloved has just been married! The anecdotal story is no hindrance to this lyrical, funny, and sad, work of art. For musical accompaniment, Kobakhidze uses a recording of Charles Aznavour ('Ekh raz, yeshcho raz') and the tune, 'Who's afraid of the big bad wolf?' from Walt Disney's *The Three Little Pigs*. The music can underline the image, be a contrast to it, be ironical about the hero, commiserate with him, or cheer him up. Kobakhidze is the first representative of cinéma d'auteur in Georgia.

An unusual comedy *Aibolit 66* (1966) has been shot by the gifted director-actor Rolan Bykov. Oleg Yefremov plays the role of a kind doctor, while the director himself plays his arch-enemy, the robber Barmaley, the villain of children's tales, despicable in his nasty ambitions. It is interesting to note that this simple fairy-tale about an animal doctor surprisingly became a very significant contribution to unusual cinematic modes of expression, for pantomime, acrobatics, actors in animal masks, a sea made with painted cloth, etc., were employed.

A re-emergence of biting satire is currently under way, e.g. *The Thirty Three* (1965) by G. Danelia, *Welcome* (1964) and *The Adventures of a Dentist* (1966) by E. Klimov. These satires are directed against crooks, bureaucrats and careerists. Klimov continues the thirties tradition of Alexander Medvedkin.

Great Comics

Eccentric elements can be found in almost all Soviet comedies on contemporary subjects in the twenties. Igor Ilyinsky – the greatest actor of the Soviet 'funnies' – looked as though he was made of different-sized balloons, with squinting eyes and a crooked head. This strange man, young in years but with old-fashioned behaviour, used to go from one misfortune to the next. His popularity was so great that he was followed by children whenever he appeared in the street. Writers and journalists have devoted libraries

Comedies

The Jolly Fellows by Grigori Alexandrov; starring Lubov Orlova

of monographs and articles to him. Like most great comics, Ilyinsky came to the cinema with stage experience. Most French and American comics came originally from the circus or vaudeville, but Ilyinsky's schooling was more extensive: from the stage dramas of the Kommissarzhevskaya Theatre and Moscow Art Theatre, to operetta and opera acting. But Ilyinsky was also the most controversial of comic actors: even his most famous films (*Aelita* (1924), *The Cigarette Girl from Mosselprom* (1924) and *The Tailor from Torzhok* (1925) all invited criticism.

One of his teachers was Vsevolod Meyerhold, but after a quarrel with him in 1935 Ilyinsky left the stage. He tried his hand at directing, but without success: his film *Once in Summer* (1936), with the inexperienced director, Shmein, was a flop. So Ilyinsky turned to acting again, using his expressive face, bull neck, funny quick gait and helpless short arms—in fact, all the features of a pig! During Stalin's time he disappeared from the screen for eighteen years, but made a come-back in 1956, adding many new roles to his career.

Another great comic was Erast Garin, also a pupil of Meyerhold's. He made his debut in the thirties in the film *Lieutenant Kizhé* (1934) and later directed and produced Gogol's *The Wedding* (1937). This later film has not survived, but according to the memories of his contemporaries, it was very impressive. Among his

Young Soviet Film Makers

St Petersburg Nights by Grigori Roshal with Lubov Orlova

most popular films are *The Musical Story* (1940), *Cain 18th* (1963) and *The Witch* (1959).

One of the most popular comediennes in Soviet cinema at that time was Lubov Orlova. In 1934 she had played her first screen role as the provincial actress, Grushenka, in Grigori Roshal's *St Petersburg Nights*. Some facets of the young actress's talent were revealed in that film—her charming sincerity, the power of her emotional expression, and her faculty for comedy in the scenes where Grushenka sings merry verses with a touching seriousness. After her great success in *Jolly Fellows*, she played many roles: songs, extravagant dances and acrobatic sketches— Orlova executed them all, directly and simply, with equal ease. She possessed a superb sense of musical rhythm and plasticity of movement.

At present one of the most popular comedians is Sergei Filippov. He was discovered by Nikolai Akimov, director of the Leningrad Theatre of Comedy, who invited the young actor to join his company. In 1937 Filippov began to act in films. His 'godfathers' here were Georgi and Sergei Vasilyev, the producers of the classic *Chapayev*. They gave Filippov a small role as a partisan in *Volochaev Days* (1937). Thereafter he quickly won a reputation as a master of comedy. If one were to observe Filippov at home, seated at his desk, preparing a current role, one would be amazed at his persistent, painstaking, literally exhausting labour. For one short sentence of dialogue he would try ten different intonations and gestures, ringing the changes, striving for perfection. Filippov is rather like a Soviet Fernandel, who by his appearance alone can have spectators aching with laughter.

The supreme clown of the Moscow circus, Yuri Nikulin, started to act in films about ten years ago, in *Girl With the Guitar* (1958). He is endearingly called 'The Fool' after the type he embodies on the screen. Like Filippov, his appearance alone brings tears of laughter. His repertoire is extensive—drunkards, vagabonds with sad eyes, cranks, petty criminals, etc.

The most interesting young comedian is Andrei Mironov. He grew up in a family of well-known cabaret artists, so he was immersed early in the entertainment business. He graduated from the Shchukin Theatre School in Moscow and later worked in the Theatre of Satire. In *Beware, the Car!* he played a black marketeer. Then he took part in the comedy *The Diamond Arm* (1970) which is being shown with great success in Moscow and where he is not only the actor, but an active participant in the whole creative process.

5 Box-Office Pictures and Actors

Although the all-important general ideological line of Soviet cinema is laid down by the State Committee of Cinematography, the commercial side is, to a certain extent, also taken into account.

Firstly, a few words about the financing of films. Every director is registered with a studio. He is on a salary, plus a percentage of the takings, depending on the rating of the film by a special commission. There are three ratings—excellent, good and satisfactory. If the film is rated unsatisfactory, it is remade (and remade) until it reaches the satisfactory level and is ready for release. As in other branches of the performing arts, a director who has distinguished himself, may receive the title of People's Artist of the Soviet Union, which means, in practical terms, that he gets a much higher salary. There is also a complicated system of prizes – the Lenin prize, Komsomol prize, etc. – which are awarded annually, and there are also many prizes connected with state holidays—Day of the Revolution, First of May, etc.

In this way the director is, on the one hand, relieved from financial worries, once his plans have been officially approved; but, on the other hand, it gives the official bodies complete control over the cinema, and no personal initiative, even as limited as the *samizdat* (or self-publishing) in literature is possible. The director can propose his own plan or can choose one of the scripts in the Script Department of the Studio. But it has happened that scripts have been more or less forced upon a director, who has to take them if he wants to do any work at all.

The release of films is the responsibility of the State Distributor, *Glavkinoprokat*, after official approval from the State Commission (the censorship), of course. Although subjects like the Revolution, the Civil War and both World Wars are traditional in Soviet cinema, the distributors (*prokatchiki*) are naturally in favour of films with a more popular appeal—love stories, comedies and adventure films. The funniest incident happened with *Ballad of a Soldier*, which the distributor did not like, because it was 'just one more film about soldiers'. It turned out to be a huge success, artistically and commercially. The subject matter was not the decisive factor; it was the individual treatment which counted here.

Among the most successful films by young directors in recent years, one must note *In Love* (1969) by the Uzbek director, Ishmukhamedov; the comedy *The Debut* (1970) by Panfilov, *The Stopwatch* (1970), a sports film by the Georgian, Esadze; and in 1971, *Sport, Sport, Sport* by the controversial director, Klimov. A few years ago a director of the middle generation, the Lithuanian Zhalakyavichus made *Nobody Wanted To Die* (1965) an adventure film on a revolutionary subject. Zhalakyavichus has openly declared that he will strive for commercial success:

'Lack of box-office success cannot leave the director unperturbed. If the people do not want to see the film, it means that the makers were unable to put their ideas into an exciting enough form. In my last film I tried not to forget this.'

Now let us look at Klimov's film, *Sport, Sport, Sport*, which is enjoying a great success with the public. First and foremost, this is a film for sports' fans, of whom there are as many in the Soviet Union as anywhere else. Secondly, it is a talented sports' feature, part cinema-interview, part documentary and part action-feature. It includes documentary excerpts of sporting events in Moscow, Philadelphia, Stockholm and Mexico, and interviews with famous sportsmen, giving fascinating biographical details. But the most interesting feature is something that has never been done before – Klimov includes old footage from the turn of the century – from the beginnings of sport. These excerpts look like the quixotic exercises of lonely heroes: even amateurs – let alone sportsmen – are now able to smile at the goings-on in those leisurely days. Klimov shows a modern sports stadium, filled with hundreds of thousands of spectators, and the utterly deserted streets of large European cities, while the events are taking place. As a featurette, he includes a re-creation of a contest famous in Russian literature —the fight between the merchant Kalashnikov, and the Tsar's *oprichnik* (bodyguard), Kiribeevich, during Ivan the Terrible's reign. The fight was filmed on the banks of the Moskva River, where such contests were actually held centuries ago. A second featurette is the life story of the sports idol of Soviet youth, Valeri Brumel, former holder of the world record in high jumping. The script of this colour film was written by a well-known sportsman, Herman Klimov, brother of the director, and no professional actors were used. It is highly regarded not only by the general public but also by sportsmen and film critics. Klimov made it with such impeccable professionalism that after the release the film attracted much attention.

The Soviet cinema also has its share of so-called 'difficult' films—that is, those which do not make enough money. Very often these are high-quality films. In the last decade these have been Kalatozov's *The Letter that Was Not Sent*, Paradzhanov's *Shadows of our Forgotten Ancestors* and *Sayat Nova*, Abuladze's *Appeal*, and Ilyenko's *On the Eve of Ivan Kupala Day*. Such films were, however, highly praised by cinema enthusiasts and some film critics, although others launched attacks on them in the press.

Success, as anywhere else, depends to a large extent, on the stars. At the beginning of the sixties, Tatiana Samoilova was especially idolised by the public. Now new names and younger people have emerged— Vertinskaya (*Hamlet* and *In Love*), Churikova (*No Ford in the Fire*, *The Debut*), Savelieva (*War and Peace*, *Sunflower*). Smoktunovsky has had a huge following for years (*Hamlet*, *Nine Days of One Year*, *Tchaikovsky*). Other successful actors are Batalov (*The Cranes Are Flying*, *Nine Days of One Year*, *The Lady With a Little Dog*), Anatoli Papanov (*In the Town of S.* and *Our House*), Rolan Bykov (*Open the Door*, *When the Bell Rings*, *Aibolit 66*, *Andrei Rublev*, *Hello, It's Me*) and Oleg Yefremov, the chief director of the Moscow 'Sovremennik Theatre' (*War and Peace*). Iya Savina, famous ten years ago for her part in Heifitz's *The Lady With a Little Dog*, is not a professional actress but a trained journalist, a graduate of Moscow University. Heifitz saw her perform at a Moscow University students' club and invited her at once to play the difficult part in the Chekhov story. Afterwards, Savina played in a rather inferior film *The Gentle Girl*, from a Dostoyevsky story. Her next role was in Mikhalkov-Konchalovsky's *Asya's Happiness*. Here her task was all the more difficult because she was playing with non-professionals, simple peasants, and had to become like these people. She managed to do so brilliantly, without the slightest trace of the exquisite 'Lady with a Little Dog'. Two further supporting roles have followed—Dolly in *Anna Karenina* and Maria Chekhova, sister of Anton Chekhov, in Yutkevich's film *Lika, Chekhov's Love (Subject For a Short Story)*.

Anastasia Vertinskaya has been very lucky in her career, achieving a most spectacular rise to fame. At the age of sixteen, she made her debut in the romance *Red Sails* (1961) and later appeared in the exotic film *The Amphibian Man* (1962). Both films were box-office hits, and Vertinskaya became famous almost overnight: her pictures appeared in magazines, she received thousands of fan letters and many offers from the best directors. Vertinskaya is the youngest daughter of the famous Russian singer, conductor, variety artist and poet Alexander Vertinsky, well-known to music-hall audiences in Europe, America and China in the twenties and thirties. In 1943, during the war, the 54-year-old emigré singer-millionaire returned to Russia with his wife, a 20-year-old painter. Vertinsky was well received in Russia, continued to appear on stage and even worked in the cinema. Anastasia Vertinskaya was born in Moscow and grew up in an artistic atmosphere. When she was a student of the Shchukin Drama School, at the Vakhtangov Theatre, she played the famous role of Ophelia in Kozintsev's *Hamlet*. Vertinskaya is like the popular idea of an actress, with her beautiful eyes, oval face, and feminine, elegant figure. In recent years she has appeared in *Anna Karenina, Cheer Up!* and *In Love*, as well as acting in productions at the Vakhtangov Theatre.

Other new actors who have recently come to the fore are Andrei Mironov, the comic (*Beware, the Car!, The Diamond Arm*), Ludmila Chursina (*The Don Story, Virineya*) and Alla Demidova (*Day's Stars, Tchaikovsky, The Seagull*).

PART II   CINEMA OF THE NATIONAL MINORITIES

6 Experiments in the Caucasus

Historical Outline—Georgia

The Georgian film industry has existed for about half a century. The natural beauty and excellent climate of this country soon attracted both Russian and foreign film makers. In the Georgian capital, Tbilisi (Tiflis), departments of the well-known firms Pathé and Filma were opened. The films made by them were mainly about the scenic beauty of the mountains and about the colourful and exotic folk festivals. Some short films for local cinemas were also made.

The first Georgian film maker was a projectionist, Alexander Digmelov, who later became a cameraman with Goskinprom studio. He started a small laboratory in 1904 and printed films, which he had shot himself, about Georgian life. Some of these reels are still available—they bear names like *The Wild Bear Hunt*, *The Funeral of the Catholicos* in Echmiadzin* and *The First Spring Races in Tbilisi*. These films were very successful with the local public in Tbilisi.

In 1910 another enthusiast made his appearance—Vassili Amushukeli, also a projectionist, from Baku, on the Caspian Sea. His productions were also of the newsreel type. Later Amushukeli went back to his native town of Kutaissi and began to shoot short films. In 1912 he made the first Georgian documentary, *The Travels of Akaki Tsereteli in Racha and Lechkhumi*: it was not a pure documentary, for scenes with acted parts were included. The story concerns the travels of a well-known Georgian poet and his encounters with the Georgian people.

In 1918 Digmelov and the owner of the cinema 'Apollo', Gegele, organised the setting up of a professional laboratory. The ownership passed to a Belgian, Pironais, who at once started to make feature films. Pironais invited Barsky, from Baku to join him and, with Digmelov on camera, they made a serialised feature entitled *The Dead Body with the Severed Head* in 1919. In the same year Pironais also produced two short films—*Tell Me Why* (*Chopin's Nocturne*) and a comedy, *Don't Sleep*. These were a commercial success and allowed the enterprising Pironais to expand his activities. Though the films made by the Pironais studio were not yet on a truly professional level, they were impressive compared with the appalling foreign productions which were usually shown in Tbilisi at that time.

In 1916 another group shot *Christine*, from the novel by E. Ninoshvili. This film was made by famous Georgian theatrical personalities (G. Gogitidze, A. Tsutsunava) and the military historian and a patron of cinema, S. Esadze. Tsutsunava wrote the script and directed the film. This comparatively large production, which was made in difficult times of war, was not a sensation but did manage to break even. The first feature film based on a Georgian script and with

---
* Head of the Armenian Church.

Georgian actors was *Arsen Georgiashvili*, released in 1920. Based on a real episode during the 1905 revolution, it concerns a Georgian revolutionary who killed the Tsarist general, Gryaznov. Mikhail Chiaureli, the leading actor, later became Stalin's favourite director, with *The Vow* (1946) and *The Fall of Berlin* (1949). As a work of art, *Arsen* was mere costume melodrama, but in historical perspective it nevertheless occupies a prominent place, since it encouraged the Georgian film makers. They at once began shooting their next film, *The Suram Castle*. Screen versions of classical Georgian literature were a most popular genre.

In 1921 the Soviet regime was established in Georgia. Amo Bek-Nazarov, Georgi Makarov, Zakhari Berishvili and Alexander Tsutsunava were among the cinema's prominent pioneers. In 1922 Georgian directors made two adaptations of works by A. Kazbegi—*The Shepherd* (1922, directed by Barsky, with Digmelov on camera) and *Patricide* (*At the Post of Shame*) (1923, director A. Bek-Nazarov, cameraman S. Zabozlaev). In 1923 Ivan Perestiani directed *The Little Red Devils*, about the romantic adventures of two boys and a girl fighting with the Red Cavalry in the Civil War. It is probably the first film in which the style of a Western is used for the treatment of a revolutionary subject. In 1924 Ivan Perestiani made another very successful film, *The Three Lives*, adapted from the novel *The First Step* by G. Tsereteli. It gives an unforgettable glimpse of *fin-de-siècle* life in Georgia, when emerging capitalism clashed with traditional feudal society. Between 1926 and 1927 Bek-Nazarov's commercial films were very popular. The lead in *Natella*, for instance, was the Georgian star Nato Vachnadze; the film is brim-full of romantic paraphernalia – harems, hot pursuits, elopements and fighting – with little or no regard for historical accuracy.

In the twenties Barsky created a film trilogy after Lermontov's *Hero of Our Time,* but its illustrative approach was rather pedestrian. Another adaptation of a classical literary work was made in 1927 – Kote Mardzhanishvili's *Stepmother Samanishvili*, a satirical comedy with talented stage actors of the realist school. In the next year or so, Mardzhanishvili made three more films – *Gogi Ratiani, Amok* and *The Gadfly* (after Lilian Voinich) – all had a fair measure of success, but were artistically inferior to *Stepmother Samanishvili.*

In the late twenties the principal theme of Georgian cinema was the 'cultural revolution'. Four young directors concentrated on this theme—Mikhail Gelovani, David Rondeli, Siko Dolidze and Leo Esakia. *Youth Conquerors* (1929), M. Gelovani's first film, scripted by G. Mdivani, is a very interesting and original film about the ancient Caucasian custom of the blood-feud (vendetta), taking place in Adzharia, where local folk customs and religious traditions are strong. In 1930, David Rondeli made his first film *Ugubziara*, also scripted by Mdivani, about the struggle against religion in a Georgian village. Siko Dolidze, in 1931, made a film, *In the Country of the Avalanches,* which was concerned with the building of the new order. Work was very difficult, shooting high in the mountains of Pshavia, not only because of natural obstacles, but also because the villagers of the mountain tribe treated the film makers with undisguised hostility: one of the actors was actually killed.

Dolidze is an ethnographer, so he could be described as the Georgian Jean Rouch. A later work – the feature *The Last Crusaders* – tells of a small Khevsurian tribe's progress towards civilisation, and explores the everyday life and customs of this tribe meticulously.

One more historical figure is widely known in

Georgian cinema—Chiaureli, who later acquired a truly unenviable reputation during the Stalin period. Chiaureli began as an interesting actor, a pupil of Ivan Perestiani. (He played the lead in *Arsen Georgiashvili* and *The Suram Castle*.) Chiaureli was educated in Moscow, where he studied painting, architecture and theatre. He worked for a time in the 'Rosta Windows' (a workshop for revolutionary propaganda posters during the Civil War) under the guidance of the famous poet, Mayakovsky. His directorial debut was in 1921, with the film *The Last Hour;* but this film disappeared without trace. In 1929 he made the rather mediocre *Saba*, a melodramatic story of a struggle against alcoholism. Not even the paintings of the Georgian genius of primitivism, Niko Pirosmanishvili, whose work is now valued at fantastic prices, could enhance the quality of this film. In 1931, with perfect timing,* Chiaureli turned his attention towards the struggle against anybody who might be in the way of the rising star of the new infallible party leader: *Khabarda!* (the Georgian expression for 'Out of the way!'). This film already had all the characteristics of a police denunciation, a feature which was to become only too familiar in all the arts under Stalin's rule. The film has the virtuous, kind and law-abiding builders of the new society opposing black villains and moral degenerates, who do all they can to undermine the progress of the country. The lasting value of the film is only that it is a reflection of the unsavoury atmosphere in Georgia (and indeed the whole of the Soviet Union) in those years, with the all-out persecution of the intelligentsia and, of course, the suppression of religion. Predictably enough, the film was noted with satisfaction in high places, and Chiaureli became a trusted man with the regime, although his reputation with the public sank to a very low level.

Among the most distinguished Georgian film makers one must note the director Nikolai Shengelaya. He came to films from literature, and wrote the script for that classic of Georgian cinema, *Stepmother Samanishvili*. In 1925 he became assistant director to Mardzhanishvili during work on the film *Before the Storm*. With the famous Russian director-cameraman, Yuri Zhelyabuzhsky, he later shot the film *Dina Dza-Dzu* in Upper Svanetia. In 1926 Shengelaya and the director, Push, were commissioned to produce *Gulli;* a newcomer to the cinema was their cameraman Mikhail Kalatozishvili, who was to achieve world fame as a director (M. Kalatozov, *The Cranes are Flying* and other films of recent years). The star of *Gulli*, Nato Vachnadze, later married Shengelaya. The film is about a Muslim girl who falls in love with a Christian from Georgia, and thereby upsets the religious fanatics of her own tribe.

In 1928 Shengelaya made his famous *Eliso*, a similarly tragic story of love between a Muslim girl and a Christian. Shengelaya's next film – the last silent film in Georgia – was *The Twenty-six Commissars*, based on events which took place in Azerbaidzhan during the Civil War. In the same year the famous Lev Kuleshov arrived in Tbilisi to make a film called *The Locomotive 1000-B*. Kuleshov, helped by the writer, critic and literary historian, Victor Shklovsky, organised lectures for young film enthusiasts. After *The Twenty-six Commissars*, Shengelaya attempted to shoot *The Virgin Soil Upturned* but, shortly after shooting began and without any explanation, it was taken out of production, and the whole team were ordered back to Tbilisi.

It is interesting to note that 1926 saw the unprece-

---

* This was the time of Stalin's triumph over Trotsky and the beginning of his absolute rule over the Communist party and the country; Stalin was a Georgian by nationality.

dented flourishing of Georgian cinema, for in that year Goskinprom released twelve full-length feature films.

The late twenties are historically connected with M. Kalatozishvili. His first important work in his native Georgia was the film *Salt for Svanetia* (Jim Shvante, 1930), a wonderful film about the struggle between man and nature. He has returned to this subject again and again in his later works.

Among the last silent films were two hilarious comedies—*Till Soon* by G. Makarov and *Zhuzhuna's Dowry* by S. Palavandishvili. Georgi Makarov was a very experienced director. His career began before the revolution, with Alexander Khanzhonkov, as an actor. Later he became an assistant to Perestiani. *Till Soon* is based on biographical facts from the life of a Georgian Bolshevik, Toma Chubinidze. It was not a serious work about revolutionary struggle in the underground movement, but a light-hearted glimpse at everyday life in Georgia at the turn of the century. The film was a huge success and stayed on Tbilisi screens for months on end.

Zhuzhuna's Dowry is another colourful comedy, about a thief who becomes the head of the collective farm stables, and out of love for the horses, tries to protect all their property against himself and his former comrades. It was a *tour de force* by the director, Palavandishvili and his last work, since he died in 1934 in tragic circumstances.

However, this was not only the transition period from silent films to talkies: two decades of Stalin's rule deeply affected the Georgian cinema. M. Chiaureli had a meteoric career under the new circumstances, while N. Shengelaya's livelihood took a turn for the worse. The first sound film by D. Rondeli, *The Cliff of Arshaul*, based on the conflict between the old and the new in the context of the industrialisation of Georgia, was less successful than S. Dolidze's experiment in sound, *The Last Crusaders*. This latter film has a clear national character, expressing the deeply ingrained and strict customs of the mountain tribes. The hero is a Khevsur peasant, a realistic, and yet a romantic figure, who has obeyed the laws of the forefathers all his life. The talented stage actor Sergo Zakariadze (who died in 1971), made his debut in this film and later became widely known through many excellent Georgian films, such as *The Father of a Soldier* (1965).

After the fiasco of *The Virgin Soil Upturned*, N. Shengelaya made *The Golden Valley*, using a totally artificial script on conventional Stalinist lines. The film about a kolkhoz village, had the standard – and, by now, obligatory – happy ending, with an apotheosis of the carefree and plentiful life in the kolkhozes. In 1939 Shengelaya made one more film in this genre, *The Fatherland*, but it was very bad indeed. Shengelaya took these misfortunes very much to heart, but there was very little he could do under the prevailing circumstances. During the early war years Shengelaya made his last film, *In the Black Mountains*, which had no redeeming qualities, and in 1943 he died at the age of forty-three.

In 1937 Chiaureli made *Arsen of Marabda*, based on a classic by M. Dzhavakhishvili, about a historical personality, the leader of a peasant revolt, but slanted to glorify the great, all-wise and beloved father of the people in the Kremlin. Thus, Chiaureli started the unending series of didactic, and immensely boring biographical and historical films, which were so characteristic of Stalin's epoch. For instance, Siko Dolidze made *Dariko*, after another nineteenth-century Georgian writer E. Ninoshvili. The novel concerns the hard life of the Georgian peasantry, and is a rather pessimistic treatment of the subject. Happiness and optimism were demanded by the authorities as a precondition for 'creativity', so the adaptation contradicted the original's intentions. Chiaureli made two thirties superproductions on revolutionary subjects—*The Last Masquerade* (1934), and *The Great Dawn* (1938). Both are clear examples of 'committed' cinema. The hero of *The Great Dawn* is a paragon of virtues, not a human being. On the strength of such characterisations, Chiaureli was invited to the Mosfilm Studios, to make *The Fall of Berlin* and *The Vow*, pompous showpieces of the cult of personality, where Stalin stems the Nazi advance by pointing his pipe at different points on the map. After 1956, when the political climate in the USSR changed, Stalin's favourite director had to return to Georgia, and his films received the critical treatment which they deserved.

In 1936 Konstantin Pipinashvili, a pupil of Eisenstein, made the beautiful children's film, *Kadzhana*, an adaptation of a novel about rural life in pre-revolutionary Georgia. *Kadzhana* left a deep impression, with its dynamic plot and vivid story of a little girl and her parents. The film was released five years late, in 1941, by which time there was a relaxation in ideological censorship. During the war Georgian cinema concentrated on solemn biographical films, whose heroes all tended to reflect the character of one man—Stalin himself. To this category belong Chiaureli's *Georgi Saakadze* (1942–3), N. Sanishvili's and I. Tumanishvili's *David Guramishvili* (1946) and David Rondeli's *Conquerors of the Peaks* (1952). The years 1945–52 were severely critical ones for Georgian cinema. Historical, biographical and even contemporary films were made according to a single formula and were completely divorced from reality. They were invariably very dull, even the formerly excellent Georgian comedies. So-called musical films emerged in their stead, built around a number of acts, with popular songs and well-known singers. All were mediocre and have disappeared into obscurity.

Armenia

The first films were shown in Armenia in 1907. During the First World War Armenian cameramen took newsreel-film of the Russo-Turkish fighting on the Caucasian front. The first Armenian film was *Under the Kurds* (1915), directed, scripted and photographed by A. Minervin.

The best Armenian silent films were based on works by classical Armenian writers, the roles being taken by well-known local stage actors. A fine feature film was *Namus*, by the outstanding Amo Bek-Nazarov, from the novel by Alexander Shirvanidze. Armenian by birth, Bek-Nazarov was a famous Russian film actor before the revolution; afterwards he worked in Georgia, then moved to the Armenian capital, Yerevan, where he made *Namus* in 1926. This film revealed his subtle talent for realism. Later works by Bek-Nazarov include *Zare* (1927), about the life of the Kurds, and *Haz-Push* (1928), a documentary on the people of Iran.

Of the silent comedies made by Armenians, *Shor and Shorshor* (1927) by Bek-Nazarov is outstanding. It is a comedy about vagabonds and layabouts. A comparably fine comedy is the satirical *The Mexican Diplomats* (1932) by A. Martirosyan and L. Kalantar, which deals with the misfortunes of two village barbers, who become 'Mexican diplomats' in a complicated intrigue. One of the last Armenian silents was a tragedy called *Gikor*, in which a village lad is apprenticed to a callous merchant.

The talkies began in Armenia with a genuine masterpiece of multinational cinema: *Pepo* (1935), directed by Bek-Nazarov, in which many famous Armenian stage actors participated. By that time, Armenia already had a number of young, talented directors, whose artistic outlook had been influenced by Eisenstein and Pudovkin. In the second half of the thirties, however, Armenian films became a faithful reflection of the general malaise in Soviet art. Even today, the majority of Armenian productions are historical-revolutionary films or features on contemporary life, such as *Hello, It's Me!* (1965) by Frunze Dovlatyan.

Azerbaidzhan
In Azerbaidzhan the cinema emerged in 1916, with Boris Svetlov in the forefront. Pre-revolutionary Azerbaidzhan cinema consisted largely of short commercial features, which had no relation to reality. From the late twenties onwards, most films made were about historical or revolutionary topics. The first of these was *In God's Name*, a propaganda film against Islam, directed by Sharif-Zade, a local actor. In 1929 the same director made *Haji-Kara*, a screen version of a classical comedy by Mirza Akhundov. In the thirties contemporary life was treated with the usual ideological slant: the struggle for the kolkhozes, the development of the oil industry, Komsomol (Young Communist) activities, and films about the unmasking of 'spies' and 'saboteurs'. In this Muslim region the question of the liberation of women from purdah was important, and it was reflected on the screen. Azerbaidzhan cinema, then, has no brilliant names nor strong local traditions to compare with the Armenian and Georgian; the local studios are small and not very well equipped.

Modern Georgia
The most interesting films in the Caucasus are now, without doubt, being made by the Georgians and are worth studying in some detail.

In the late fifties and sixties Gruzia Film Studios

White Caravan by Eldar Shengelaya

produced many original films which enjoy great and deserved popularity at home and on the international market. Among them are such unusual films as Tengiz Abuladze and Rezo Chkheidze's *Lurdzha Magdany* (1955), which continued the best traditions of Georgian cinema of the twenties and thirties, and received the Grand Prix in Cannes; also *I, Grandma, Iliko and Illarion* (1963) by Tengiz Abuladze; Rezo Chkheidze's *The Father of a Soldier* (1965); *The White Caravan* (1964) by Eldar Shengelaya; Shota Managadze's *Khevsur Ballad* (1967); Georgi Shengelaya's *He Did Not Want to Kill* (1969); Georgi Danelia's *Cheer Up!* (1969); and the fine document-

Experiments in the Caucasus

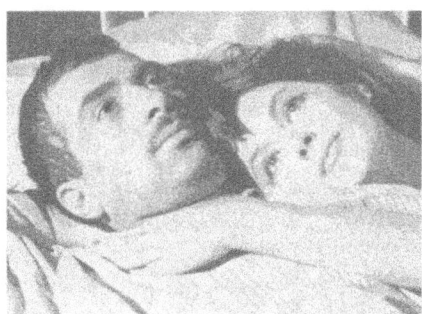

White Caravan by Eldar Shengelaya

White Caravan by Eldar Shengelaya

aries of George Asatiani. Young and gifted film makers have shot some very impressive short films: M. Kokochashvili's *The Old Beech* (1957), a very original and romantic work; G. Shengelaya's controversial film *Allaverdoba* (1962); O. Yoseliani's 20-minute documentary *Cast Iron* (1964) made with a hidden camera; E. Shengelaya's sombre *Mikela* (1964); and M. Kobakhidze's charming short films *The Wedding* (1965), *The Umbrella* (1967) and *The Musicians* (1970). All the films by these young Georgian directors are real works of art: the subject matter is usually drawn from local life.

. The brothers Georgi and Eldar Shengelaya are part of a family, which is at the very centre of Georgian cinema—their father, Nikolai Shengelaya, was one of the pioneers of film making in Georgia, and their mother, Nato Vachnadze, was the first Georgian film star. The brothers both graduated from the VGIK. Georgi started as an actor and appeared in many Georgian films. His first feature, *Allaverdoba* (1967), based on a short film which he made while still at the Institute in 1962, shows how every autumn the local people descend from the mountains to the ancient church 'Allaverdy' for the traditional Thanksgiving Day. 'Allaverdoba' is the multitude of people who eat, drink dance and make merry. Since this is a religious holiday, the film was presumed to be anti-religious, but when it was completed, the religious elements of the ceremony stood out so strongly that the film aroused sharp controversy in the press. After the intercession of the highly regarded author and critic V. Shklovsky, who wrote: 'to be afraid of religious ecstasy and an ancient faith at the present day is like to be afraid of the secession of the Vladimir-Suzdal principality from Russia'—the critics decided to classify the film as harmless. It was even stated that the film has its required anti-religious contents, because, after all, the hero disapproves of all the wild drinking that is going on. The director's method is to set exquisite satirical mini-portraits against a documentary background; and the result is a kaleidoscope of Georgian life.

Two years later, Georgi Shengelaya made an adventure film *Matsy Khvitiya* (*He Did Not Want To Kill*), full of passionate, Caucasian style scenes. Still, after *Allaverdoba* it was, in a way, a step backwards, a relinquishing of the subtle psychological approach of the former film in favour of what amounts to commercial cinema.

In 1970 Georgi Shengelaya made another feature, *Pirosmani*, about the life of the almost legendary Georgian primitivist painter Niko Pirosmanishvili, who died of starvation at the age of sixty, in 1918. The scriptwriters, Georgi Shengelaya and Erlom Akhvled-

Matsy Khvitia (*He Did Not Want To Kill*) by Georgi Shengelaya

iani, had a very difficult task, because so few biographical details are known about the painter—even in his native Kakhetia nobody knows where his grave is, and his few remaining contemporaries say that he was a rather strange and lonely man who had few close friends. As it cannot be an accurate biographical portrayal, the film is centred on Pirosmani's work: the designers, A. Varazishvili and V. Arabidze, recreated the quaint atmosphere of the painter's world. One of the designers, Avtandil Varazishvili, also plays the part of Pirosmani.

The film consists of several parts—'Giraffe', 'White Cow', 'Easter Lamb', 'Count', and 'Yellow Lion'—which are linked by the story of two painters—Zdanevich and Le Dantu—who come from Petersburg to Tiflis to find Pirosmani.

Eldar Shengelaya, a pupil of Sergei Yutkevich, graduated from the VGIK as a director in 1958. Eldar's approach is more lyrical than his brother's. This might be due to the influence of Dovzhenko, who was one of his teachers. *The White Caravan*, a film about the generation gap which attracted much attention when it appeared, was made by Eldar Shengelaya in collaboration with Tamaz Meliava. The hero, the son of a herdsman, does not want to follow in his father's footsteps. Eldar Shengelaya's best film, however, is undoubtedly the short *Mikela*, one of three parts of the compilation film *Pages of the Past* (1964), the brothers Shengelaya and Merab Kokochashvili each contributing an episode. *Mikela* is the dramatic story of a lonely old man, whose whole family is being wiped out, one by one, by some unknown and fatal disease, and who now desperately tries to save his only surviving grandson from the same tragic fate. The film, full of brooding fatalism, has a haunting atmosphere of unavoidable doom.

In 1969 Eldar Shengelaya made the feature *Love,*

Dagger and Treason, a tragicomedy, similar to the *Naples Millionaire (Napoli Millionaria).*

Otar Yoseliani is currently regarded as one of the most significant Georgian directors. He was a professional musician for a time, after five years' study of the piano, composition and conducting at the Tbilisi Music School. He was also a professional painter, and he devoted five years to study in the mechanics and mathematics department of Moscow University, but just before taking exams he switched over to the directors' faculty of the VGIK. At the cinema institute he studied under Dovzhenko and made a short, *Watercolour* (1958). His first feature film was the amazing *April (Stories About Things)* (1961). The story is very simple. There are two people in a new house, in a completely empty room. Without talking, they can understand each other, just by glances: they are very happy. But gradually a cupboard, then a chair, a table, bowls, napkins, etc. appear and slowly the people are enslaved by their things. Their love falls to pieces.

April is a cinematic fairy tale built up on the contrast between dreams and the drab reality of life. The idea was to show how daily routine frustrates feelings, to show the importance of defending the spiritual in life. Yet, for absolutely inexplicable reasons, the film was not passed for general release. In despair, Yoseliani decided to give up film making, he went to a factory as a worker, and a few months later became a sailor and went to sea. On his return, however, he could not stay away from the camera. He made a documentary, *Cast Iron,* which can be regarded in many ways as a training exercise and an echo of a masterpiece such as *The Salt for Svanetia,* an early film by Mikhail Kalatozov. *Cast Iron* was shot with a hidden camera at the Rustavi Metallurgical Works, in Georgia.

The lessons he learnt are fully assimilated in his

next feature *When Leaves Fall* (1967, awarded the George Sadoul prize in 1970) which is shot in a documentary style, similar to Marlen Khutsiev's films and Georgi Shengelaya's *Allaverdoba*. The Georgian director Khutsiev, working at Mosfilm Studios in the early sixties, caused a storm of controversy with his *I Am Twenty* (*Ilyich Square*). It was deeply concerned with contemporary problems, and his highly individual approach gave him the reputation of being close to Italian neo-realism. Khutsiev is occupied with the problems of contemporary youth in general, whereas Shengelaya and Yoseliani discuss only problems of national Georgian character.

When Leaves Fall is a study of present-day society with all its problems, troubles, frustrations and contradictions. Yoseliani shows the Georgian capital, Tbilisi, without a romantic glow, using a hidden camera and microphone. A wine distillery tries to overfulfill the plan – the main aim of every enterprise in the Soviet economy – by tampering with the quality of the wine. Friends and relatives visit the place, as if it were their own wine cellar; the director spends days playing billiards. Nobody seems to notice the sorry state of affairs, either because it suits them, or simply through carelessness. The hero, a shy youngster who unexpectedly turns out to be highly principled and unyielding, tries to put things right and gets himself into a fix. As a last resort, he adopts the manners of his enemies – swears, gives orders, swindles – and gets his way. The film consists of episodes, named after days of the week, but not in chronological order.

Mikhail Kobakhidze has an unusual talent. He makes incomparably aesthetic featurettes, which are delicate in form and fantastic in character. Kobakhidze's diploma work was his short *The Wedding* (1965), which was singled out for the Grand Prix at Oberhausen. In it he used a modern version of the

When Leaves Fall by Otar Yoseliani

silent comedy traditions: the film shows the comic hero's despair when his fiancée marries someone else, and its sad humour is exquisite.

The Wedding was actually Kobakhidze's third short: as a VGIK student he made *Young Love*, in which a geologist, returning from an expedition, plays a trick on his wife but it rebounds and he becomes the victim; and *The Merry-go-round* (1962), about a young man excited by a forthcoming rendezvous.

Kobakhidze's next short, *The Umbrella* (1967) won the Grand Prix at the Cracow short film festival in the same year. It is another comical pantomime with a Georgian background. An umbrella travels through

Experiments in the Caucasus

When Leaves Fall by Otar Yoseliani

the air to listen to peoples' music and to have a closer look at human beings. Kobakhidze's technique has evolved further: movement acquires special importance here, and he takes infinite care to achieve the exact expressions; he always selects the music (the soundtrack) himself, thus creating a sense of perfect unity. His films are mini-masterpieces. In 1970, Kobakhidze made a 15-minute film, *The Musicians*, which in contrast to his previous shorts, dispenses with story-line altogether, and becomes a gay improvisation, a dance which gradually envelops people and even things.

Merab Kokochashvili is a descendant of one of the greatest Georgian classical writers, Ilya Chavchavadze. He came into films from the VGIK in 1958. He then became interested in the Georgian countryside and produced a fine sketch of village life, *Mikha* (1964), which was included in the film *Pages of the Past*. It is the traditional story of a girl who loves a poor young lad, but her parents try to marry her off to a rich man. It is presented in a colourful folk context. According to local customs, a girl who spends the night with a man before her wedding day, can only belong to him, and nobody else. The lovers take advantage of this custom and barricade themselves in, and although the despairing relatives put up a regular siege, they are

75

Young Soviet Film Makers

Georgian comedy-maker Mikhail Kobakhidze

forced to admit defeat in the end. The film has a marvellous sense of humour.

Kokochashvili's second film about rural life was the full-length feature *The Wide Green Valley* (1967). It tells how an old shepherd fights desperately against the encroachment of the city, against machines and all that endangers the wide green valley, where his forefathers have tended their flocks for centuries. The hopelessness of his last stand in defence of nature, in this technological age gives the film a great feeling of tragedy.

Kokochashvili has also made a short, *From House*

to House (1961) with director Otar Abesadze based on a story by the Georgian writer, David Kldiashvili. Their pathetic hero is delicately sketched and they show clear insight about his tragicomic situation. One watches him with mingled pity and amusement, sympathy and indignation. A kind but amazingly inept blunderer, he has managed in his lifetime to lose everything he ever possessed, yet he is firmly convinced that the noble are not born to earn their bread by the sweat of their brows, least of all, by tilling the soil. So, hungry but proud, Solomon, the zealous matchmaker, goes from house to house arranging marriages in the hope that parents will shower gold and silver into his eager palms. Tricked by all, ill-treated by fortune, and none the richer, he stands in his worn but showy Georgian *cherkeska* at the loaded wedding table, trying not to betray his sadness to his tormentors. He climbs on his donkey and trails off home, only to meet his implacable creditors. Seeing them, the old man, in fear and despair, turns the animal around and gallops away into the distance.

After this film Otar Abesadze shot the feature *The Spring Will Come Soon*. The script was partly written by the director, Otar Yoseliani: it dealt with real problems of village life and villagers, using the dramatic situation of an old peasant abandoned by his children.

Georgi Kalatozishvili, a son of Mikhail Kalatozov, graduated from the VGIK as a cameraman. In 1958 he went to the North Pole and shot *Two Captains*, in very harsh conditions, for the Lenfilm studio. Thereafter he worked for Gruzia Films, doing the lighting on *I, Grandma, Iliko and Illarion; The White Caravan;* and *I See the Sun*. Recently Kalatozov Jr. has turned to directing *Death of a Philatelist* (1971), a commercial thriller.

Pavel Arsenov came from Tiblisi, graduated from the VGIK, and started at the Gorky Studio. *The Sunflower*, from Vitali Zakrutkin's story of a true incident during the war, concerns the herdsmen of the Kalmyk steppe, their customs, and the beauty of their homeland. An old shepherd grows a sunflower from a seed he finds in the pocket of his son, who was killed in the war; and the flower becomes a symbol of the indestructibility of life. After *The Sunflower* Arsenov made another short, *Lelka* (1967), about the first romance of a 15-year-old girl, which was full of warmth and humour. In 1971, Arsenov shot the feature *King-Deer*, adapted from the famous play by Carlo Gozzi. The film was shot on location in the Crimea, and has preserved the theatrical conventions of the fairy-tale.

Another young Georgian director is Gela Kandelaki. His extraordinary documentary, *Quiet Long Melody* (1966), deals with the reminiscences of an old peasant about his hard life, against the backdrop of a contemporary Georgian village.

Rezo Esadze came into films from science—he was a college teacher in physics and astronomy. At the VGIK Esadze studied under Mikhail Romm. In 1963, while still a student, he made the short, *Once*, which aroused controversy at the Institute. It was a complex picture, and showed signs of his search for an individual style of expression. Esadze's diploma work was another short, *Fro* (1965), adapted from a psychological story by a well-known and controversial Soviet writer, Andrei Platonov, whose works were only published after Stalin's death.

Fro is about the mad love of a young woman, Frosya, for her husband, who is helping to build the new life. The film is set in the thirties, and it established Esadze's reputation; but his next film, also shot at the Lenfilm Studio, *Four Pages of a Young Life* (1967), a feature about contemporary Soviet

Young Soviet Film Makers

Four Pages From A Young Life by Rezo Esadze

youth, turned out to be too long and amorphous, and it must be considered a failure.

His 1970 feature, *The Stopwatch*, is about a football idol who reaches the advanced age of thirty-five, and must retire. A commercial picture, it is aimed at the vast numbers of football fans in the Soviet Union.

One of the most significant Georgian directors is Georgi Danelia. In his early youth he was a member of a jazz band, and later graduated and worked as an architect. Then suddenly he became captivated by the cinema and attended the two-year directors' course at Mosfilm studios. His diploma work was the short *They Are Also People* (1959, in collaboration with I. Talankin), an episode from Tolstoy's *War And Peace*.

Danelia's first full-length feature *Splendid Days* (*Seryozha*) made in 1960, again in collaboration with Talankin, was a brilliant debut: it was awarded three international prizes—in Mexico, in Vancouver and at Karlovy Vary. It tells the story of a 5-year-old boy getting a new stepfather; but it is the child's story, and is seen through his eyes.

Danelia's next film, *The Way to the Wharf* (1962) was not of the same standard. In attempting a psychological study, the director slipped into banalities: in a later interview he disowns this film.

I Walk About Moscow (1963) was a successful comedy, shot by Vadim Yusov, who was already well-known in his own right. Danelia has said about this film: 'It is not a slice of life, nor a newsreel. It is a modern fairy-tale with noble heroes and beautiful fairies. Indeed, if you look, all my films are to some extent fairy-tales. . . .'

This might be true, but one of his films does not

Experiments in the Caucasus

Stopwatch by Rezo Esadze

Stopwatch by Rezo Esadze

Young Soviet Film Makers

seem to fit this description. Not many people have had an opportunity to see it, as the film was not passed by the censor: *The Thirty-Three* gave Danelia his reputation as an 'angry' director. This comedy, shot in 1965, is about sensationalism in the mass-media. Had it been set in a Western country there would have been no trouble whatsoever with censorship. But the film shows that socialist society is also riddled with sensationalism, and the powers-that-be felt they must suppress this idea—and the film was banned.

The film deals with a young dentist who unexpectedly discovers thirty-three teeth in the mouth of a perfectly ordinary Soviet citizen: that is, one more than everybody else has. The man becomes a celebrity overnight, journalists follow him wherever he goes, radio and television ask for interviews and opinions, beautiful girls instantly fall in love with him. The hero travels around quite a lot, and this gives the director an opportunity to present a whole gallery of the *bêtes noires* of Soviet society. The censor sensed subversion and disrespect for the authorities, so the film is still gathering dust on a shelf.

Danelia's most recent work is the colour film *Cheer Up!* (1969) from the French novel *Mon Oncle Benjamin* by Claude Tillier. The action has been transplanted to Georgia at the beginning of the twentieth century. The camera is again in the capable hands of V. Yusov, who is without doubt the best cameraman in Soviet cinema at present.

The Thirty Three by Georgi Danelia (Inna Churikova and Yevgeni Leonov)

7 The Lithuanian Film Studio

Lithuanian cinematography is currently regarded as one of the most interesting regional industries. The first films were shown in Lithuania in 1898 by foreign cinema companies. By 1905 the first permanent cinema had been opened in Kaunas (Kowno). The first Lithuanian cameraman was A. Rachunas, a resident of the USA but a regular visitor to Lithuania, where he shot landscapes and scenes from everyday life. He would project these reels to the colonies of homesick Lithuanian emigrés in America. Newsreel and documentary cinema also became well developed in Lithuania thanks to A. Rachunas, P. Milus, G. Klimas and others, but their films were still rather amateurish at this stage.

During the years 1926–9 various studios and filmschools appeared, such as the Studio of Drama and Ballet, Studio Glass, and so on. The famous theatrical personality, I. Vaichkus (of Hollywood fame) founded a studio which prepared actors for the national cinema in Lithuania. Unfortunately it did not last long, because of financial difficulties. The first Lithuanian feature, *Onite and Ionelis*, directed by F. Dunayevas and Y. Lenartas, appeared in 1931. It was about a young couple who leave their native village to try their luck in the town. In the lead were three famous stage actors of the day—V. Fedotovas, A. Letuvaite and P. Pinkauskaite.

The Lithuanian film studio was founded in 1949, so it is still young, but its productions have received widespread recognition in the Soviet Union. Its first film, *Marite*, was rather weak; and others made during the first decade were merely attempts, but the later films can be called achievements: *Adam Wants To Be a Man* (1959), *Ignotas Came Back Home* (1960), *Footsteps in The Night* (1962), *The Girl and the Echo* (1964) and *Chronicle of One Day* (1964). Two isolated successes were the film, *Living Heroes* (1959), made by Bratkauskas, Zhebrunas, Zhalakyavichus and Gedris which won the Grand Prix at the twelfth International Film Festival in Karlovy Vary in 1960; and a commercial and popular thriller, *Nobody Wanted To Die*, by Zhalakyavichus.

In recent years three hitherto forbidden themes have emerged in Lithuanian cinema—the occupation of the Baltic countries by the Red Army on the eve of the Second World War; the re-occupation during the drive towards Germany which is officially called 'the period of the establishment of Soviet power'; and also the return, after Stalin's death, of many people deported to Siberia after the war. Stalin annexed the Baltic countries, with Hitler's connivance, in 1939. The people themselves put up bitter resistance, but partisan fighting against the imposed order was, as usual in such cases, brutally crushed by the secret police with the help of local communists. Lithuanian film makers had to present this period within the

Young Soviet Film Makers

official perspective, of course.

Vitautas Zhalakyavichus is a leading Lithuanian director with a vivid modern approach. He started with a commercial thriller *Adam Wants To Be a Man* (1959). The action takes place in independent Lithuania. A young worker is unemployed and dreams of emigrating to Buenos Aires. When at last he scrapes together the money needed for his ticket, the manager of the travel office flees abroad himself, taking all the money with him, and also the unfortunate worker's girl-friend.

In 1960 Zhalakyavichus directed the last episode of *Living Heroes*, with the same title. The film consists of four independent episodes as dissimilar in style as are the professional careers of their respective directors. The other episodes (under the general direction of Zhalakyavichus) were made by 24-year-old Marionas Gedris, a graduate of the VGIK; Balis Bratkauskas, a leading actor at the Vilnius Theatre of Drama; and Arunas Zhebrunas, an architect and artist. The four episodes are, however, unified by their theme – childhood – which should be happy, but often is not.

Zhalakyavichus' next film was *Nobody Wanted To Die* (1964). The events depicted took place during the early post-war years. The 'men in the woods', as the partisans who went to the forests were called, have killed a local communist, the chairman of the Village Council. A struggle develops between those who do not want the communist regime and the sons of the murdered communist who helped to establish the 'new life' in their country. The victory of the new life claims many victims, but nobody wanted to die. . . . This tragic story is extremely gory and violent: there is a great deal of shooting and the tension typical of a thriller, yet the film is also deeply psychological.

The Chronicle of One Day (made in 1963, but not

Adam Wants to Be a Man by Vitautas Zhalakyavichus

Summer of Men by Marionas Gedris

released until the end of 1964) aroused controversy because it showed one of the unprincipled careerists in conflict with the extreme indignation of the people. The young cameraman Araminas displayed some new and fascinating techniques.

The first episode of *Living Heroes* is by the young director, Gedris, and is called *We Do Not Need Anyone Now*. It is set in the twenties and tells the story of a little boy. The boy's parents have decided to send him to work for a rich farmer, herding stock. There is nothing to eat at home and the boy regards the new venture with a mixture of sorrow and pride. He is to become a bread-winner. But when he arrives, the landlord drives him out, saying: 'We do not need anyone now.' This short, very human story is melancholy but fascinating.

In the same style, the romantic film *The Girl and The Echo* was made about a child, a girl who collected echoes on the beach. Made in 1965 by Arunas Zhebrunas, it won prizes at Locarno and at Cannes.

Later Zhebrunas shot two other romantic films: *The Little Prince* (1967), Lithuania's only colour film, an adaptation of Antoine de St-Exupéry's *Le Petit Prince;* and *The Beautiful Girl* (1969). *The Little Prince* is not very successful. The ironic charm of the original has largely disappeared and the screen version

Lithuanian director Vitautas Zhalakyavichus directing *Nobody Wanted to Die*

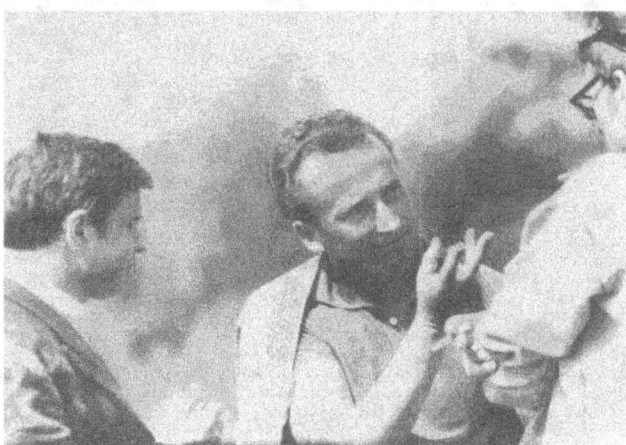

Young Soviet Film Makers

Nobody Wanted to Die by Vitautas Zhalakyavichus

The Chronicle of One Day by Vitautas Zhalakyavichus

is deadly serious, pompous and didactic. The gently melancholic dreams of the book have been transformed into a series of dead-pan tricks.

The Beautiful Girl is about a plain 9-year-old girl with a rich 'inner world'. The part was played by a 10-year-old schoolgirl from Kaunas, Inga Mitskite, who cleverly expressed all the female emotions on her freckled face. We see her almost adult agony when the other children – as prearranged – elect her Beauty Queen, so that she must dance while they praise her appearance. Suddenly a strange boy appears and, with the mischievous cruelty typical of children, tells Inga flatly that she is not beautiful at all, but very ugly.

The film's main subjects – imagined beauty and loneliness – are embodied in this child actress.

Zhebrunas directed the third episode of *Living Heroes* under the title of *The Last Shot*. An anti-Soviet partisan in the aftermath of the war is surprised in his hide-out by a small girl. Fearing detection he kills her, but an enraged mob kill him. *The Last Shot* is a good example of a film committed to the official line despite its romantic disguise. It shows again that a director's talent can be as undeniable as his intentions are dubious.

Raimondas Vabalas began with a commercial war film *Footsteps in the Night* (1963), about the Nazi

The Lithuanian Film Studio

The Girl and the Echo by Arunas Zhebrunas

occupation of Lithuania in 1943. His second film, *March, March, Boom-Boom-Boom!* (1964) features a pompous martinet, a kind of Napoleon *manqué*, in a 'comedy grotesque' set in the thirties, during the local Ruritania-style war between Poland and Lithuania. This fast-moving film includes excerpts from Polish and Lithuanian newsreels of that period. Vabalas' third film is *Stairs to the Sky* (1966) based on the novel of the same name by Mikolas Slutskyus. In the years immediately after the war, a country family whose head does not believe in the new life yet sees the old world in ruins, comes to a tragic end. Vabalas, on the strength of this sombre film, is now one of the most highly-regarded directors in Lithuania.

When I Was Young (1969) made by director-cameraman Araminas, is a screen version of a work by the young Estonian writer, Mati Unt: *Red Cat, Good-Bye!*, written when he was eighteen years old. In his poetic and wistfully ironic film, Araminas deals with the difficult subject of first love between pupils at grammar school, as well as saying something about loneliness and the psychology of young people.

The Beautiful Girl by Arunas Zhebrunas

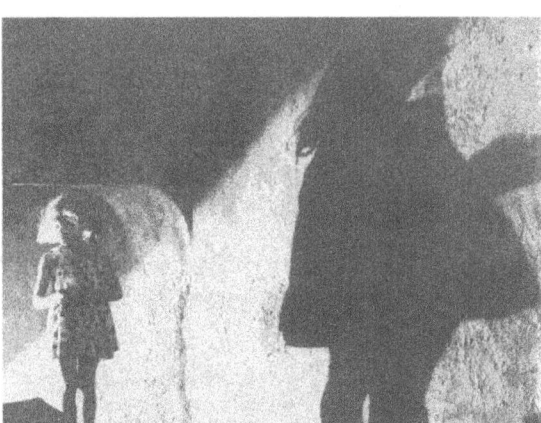

The Last Shot—the last episode from *Living Heroes*

Living Heroes directed by V. Zhalakyavichus, M. Gedris, B. Bratkausas, A. Zhebrunas

Footsteps in the Night by Raimondas Vabalas

8 Moldavian Cinema

The Moldavian Film Studio was set up fifteen years ago, so it is one of the youngest in Russia. The studio's first film to win widespread popularity was *Chieftain Kodr* (1958), an epic about a Moldavian national hero. The films *Lullaby* (1960) and *Man Following the Sun* (1961) by Mikhail Kalik, and *The Last Month of Autumn* (1965) by Vadim Derbenev have won a prominent place in contemporary Soviet cinema. These films were singled out for commendation at the international film festivals at Locarno, Mar-del-Plata and Cannes.

Moldova Film-Studio productions have a truly national flavour, reflecting the everyday life, customs, traditions and art of Moldavia. The emphasis on youth largely accounts for the intensive experimentation, the desire to master everything new that emerges in world cinematography.

Vadim Derbenev, a graduate from the camera department of the VGIK, began work at the Moldova Film-Studio with the freshness and originality of a major talent. *Chieftain Kodr* and later *Lullaby* displayed his impressive camerawork—a riot of rich, striking and unexpected colour; but there was more to come. When his *Man Following the Sun* was released we saw a poem of beauty; and in 1963, Derbenev took the crucial step and tried his hand at directing.

Journey into April was his first venture as a director. One may argue about the film's merits and demerits, but one thing is unquestionable—Derbenev remains true to his conception of beauty. In *The Last Month of Autumn* (scripted by Ion Drutse) he draws a symbolic parallel between the last month of autumn, when the harvest has been safely gathered in, and the autumn of life.

Two other young Moldavian film makers, the director Vadim Lysenko and the scriptwriter Valeri Gazhiu, came to the Moldova Film-Studio after graduating from the VGIK, starting their work with the film, *When Storks Fly Away* (1964), about a lonely old farmer.

Their next most important feature was *Bitter Grains* (1967). The film shows the difficulties and conflicts that arise before the Moldavian peasants can settle down to a peaceful life after liberation from the Nazis. One feels that the very first shots will be a portent of all that follows, for the film opens with the execution of Soviet paratroopers captured by the Nazis. The execution takes place against the walls of a barn where grain is stored. After passing through human bodies, the bullets drill holes in the side of the barn. And from these terrifying punctures, streams of wheat pour down onto the heads of the fallen men, filling their eye-sockets, covering their mouths, packing their ears, and strewing their hair. Again the shots ring out, again the grain trickles, this time from new holes, onto the faces of the victims. Apart from

Young Soviet Film Makers

Journey into April by Vadim Derbenev

its overpowering symbolism, the execution scene is an effective introduction to the hard life experienced by one Moldavian village after the war, and to the otherwise 'realistic' portrayal of their traditional dress, household utensils and their celebrations and ceremonies which have developed over the centuries.

The Red Glades (1966) by a young Moldavian director Emil Lotyanu is an exotic colour film about the Bessarabian shepherds, their songs, dances and customs, their loves and hates, their tenderness and kindness, cruelty and justice.

In 1971 Lotyanu made *The Leutary*. In former times, the colourful tribe of Leutary (Bessarabian gipsies) – vagrant musicians and singers – lived in Moldavia. The Leutary were virtuosi on many instruments and created a musical folklore, which is still alive among musicians today. They travelled all over Europe and gave successful performances in Paris, St Petersburg and Vienna. Yet, strange as it seems, their art was regarded with suspicion at home; and at the end of the nineteenth century the tribe disappeared. The hero of the film is the Leutar, Thoma Alistar, famous in Moldavia for centuries. All Alistars were brilliant musicians, but Thoma was the best of them. This romantic adventure is not only about Thoma's talent, but also about his great passions, and his

Moldavian Cinema

The Leutary by Emil Lotyanu

The Leutary by Emil Lotyanu

Young Soviet Film Makers

The Leutary by Emil Lotyanu

tremendous love for Lyanka. Their lives have a tragic end. In this film music naturally plays an important part, with both the original songs and melodies of the Leutary, and the best Moldavian musicians of the day – Kharlampi Berdaga, Lubomir Iorga and Nikolai Fagurel – featured.

9 The Awakening of the Steppes

The oldest cinematic traditions in Soviet Central Asia are those of the Uzbek. The first films were shown in Tashkent in 1897. In 1924 the Russo-Bukhar company, Bukhkino, was founded. Among the pictures released by this organisation, *The Muslim Woman* and *The Minaret of Death* (both in 1925) were made by Russian directors and cameramen. In 1925 the Uzbekgoskino studio was formed, and a sizeable film industry was initiated. N. Ganiev became its first director and actor. From 1926 the studio presented mostly documentaries and popular scientific films. During the era of silent pictures, well-known Russian directors and cameramen worked in Uzbekistan—O. Freilikh, K. Gertel, M. Doronin, F. Verigo-Darovsky and others; and Uzbek cinematographers also started to work, including K. Yarmatov, N. Ganiev and N. Khodzhaev. The first Uzbek sound film, *The Vow* (1937, director A. Usoltsev-Garf), was about collectivisation, and was made to the rigid formula prevalent at that time. During the war many of the central studios were evacuated to Uzbekistan, and films like *Nasreddin in Bukhara* (by Y. Protazanov), *Two Soldiers* and *Alexander Parkhomenko* (by L. Lukov) were made. In the fifties didactic and historical-biographical films prevailed in Uzbekistan, as everywhere else—*Avicenna* (1957), directed by Yarmatov, for instance. In other republics of the region – in Tadzhikistan and Turkmenistan – cinematography was undeveloped, studios lacked equipment and only produced one or two films a year, and these were mainly made by Russian film makers.

The Kazakhfilm studio was created during the Second World War out of the Alma-Ata Documentary film studios where Eisenstein had made his *Ivan the Terrible*. The Uzbekfilm and the Kirghizfilm studios were founded in 1961. In previous years Kirghiz film makers had made joint productions with the film makers of Moscow, Leningrad and Kazakhstan, but in the sixties a large group of first-class national film makers graduated from the VGIK, including young Uzbeks, Kazakhs and Kirghizs, directors, scriptwriters and cameramen, who have now become familiar names in the Soviet cinema. The documentary *Manaschi* (1966) made by Bolot Shamshiev, won several international prizes. At the Kirghizfilm studio an interesting two-part short, *Sandcastle* (1967), was made by A. Vidugiris and Y. Bronstein: it won the international prize at the Cracow Festival in 1968. *Sandcastle* is about a little boy who makes fantastic sandcastles on the beach. It is half-documentary, with many touching details, charming music and an interesting style of editing.

Even a few years ago, studios barely managed to make one or two films a year. But in 1969 Uzbekfilm studio made six films, and four of these were by young directors.

Young Soviet Film Makers

Tolomush Okeev is the first director in modern Kirghiz cinema. Having returned from Leningrad, where he graduated at the cinema engineers' institute, he worked as a sound recordist at Kirghizfilm studio, notably on Shepitko's *Heat*, which is now considered a classic in its field. The counterpoint texture of musical melody, the thunder of hooves and the singing of women against the background of roaring tractors, was made with immense professional skill. In 1964, Okeev joined the directors' course at the Mosfilm studio. As a student he prepared a short *These Are Horses* (1965), which won a number of awards abroad. This film shows the life cycle of horses: an awkward new-born foal; a noosed horse in the wild steppe; breaking in with lashes of the whip; the excitement of races, shouting crowds; and then the last journey to the slaughterhouse, and tears in the eyes of other old horses. In just ten minutes Okeev manages to create a deep impression.

Two years later he made his first feature in Kirghizia *The Sky of Our Childhood* (1967), which won a prize at the Frankfurt Festival. The subject is deeply autobiographical. A 10-year-old boy arrives by plane from the city on a visit to his parents, who live in the Kirghizian mountains, just across the border from Sinkiang. Okeev himself spent his childhood on the grasslands between the majestic snowy peaks of Tien Shan, where his father and grandfather used to rear horses, the pride of this country. Just like his hero, Okeev became very familiar with every aspect of horse-rearing, and at the age of ten left for the city school. His film is a memorial to a vanishing world, a requiem and a cry of anguish. Okeev himself said in an interview:

The Sky of Our Childhood by Tolomush Okeev

The Sky of Our Childhood by Tolomush Okeev

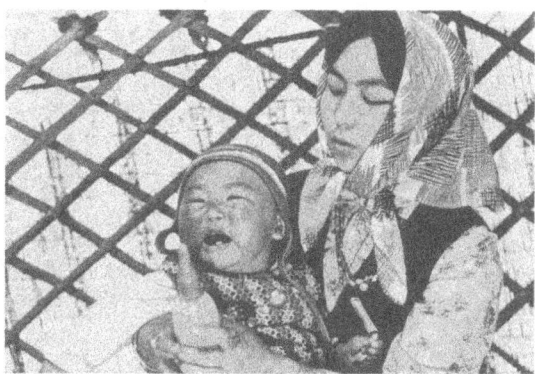

'I want to preserve the memory of the last of our clans. They gave us food and clothing. We often ridicule our old men and boast of our modern ways. But thinking it over, I am sure that there are things we could learn from them. They do not drink, do not smoke, are not mercenary and they never lie. They seem to belong purely to nature, which is all around them....'

The preparation of *The Sky of Our Childhood* was extremely painstaking. Various techniques of shooting herds of galloping horses had to be tried out and the principles of wide angle photography explored in practice. Equally thorough are his short called *Boom*, about the Boom mountain pass in Kirghizia, his scripts and his feature *The Heritage* (1970). *The Heritage* is presented as the dialogue of an old man on the verge of death with his wife, who is waiting at the doors of the hospital to hear the result of an operation.

Another prominent young director from Kirghizia is Bolot Shamshiev, also a VGIK graduate. He played the lead in Shepitko's *Heat* when he was still at the Film Institute. Two years later his diploma work, *Manaschi* (1966), won a prize at Oberhausen. In it Shamshiev, like his countryman Okeev, turns to Kirghizia's history and its folk-legends. In 1967, Shamshiev made a second short, *The Herdsman*, concerning man's struggle with the elements. In the mountain world of Kirghizia a lonely herdsman is constantly on the look-out. There is a splendid sequence showing the descent from the mountain, with herdsmen moving at terrific speed, and the

Young Soviet Film Makers

clouds they encounter masking the difficulty of the downward journey. Equally brilliant are the static shots and close-ups: the deep wrinkles, the large, heavy hands of the man. The story, then, is in a documentary style.

Shamshiev's first full-length feature is *Gunshot at the Mountain Pass* (1969), another picture about his country's past, dealing with the life of a horse-thief, a lonely and generous man who is forced by circumstances to become a robber and an outcast. The colourful life of pre-revolutionary Kirghizia unfolds on the screen—the silken robes of the local princes,

The Gunshot at the Mountain Pass by Bolot Shamshiev

The Gunshot at the Mountain Pass by Bolot Shamshiev

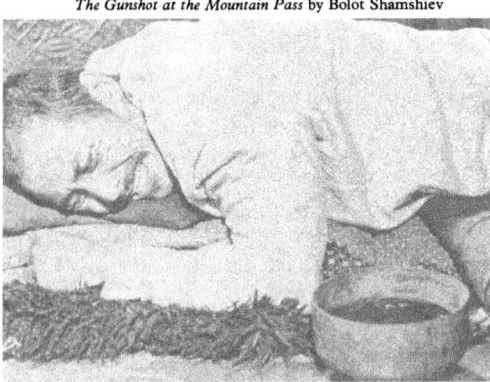

The Awakening of the Steppes

The Curse by Bolot Shamshiev

The Curse by Bolot Shamshiev

wonders of horsemanship, Kazakh refugees from China, Russian settlers, the Old Believer,* Cossacks, and many more. The re-creation of times past has a very genuine flavour. Two-thirds of the film was shot on location—at a high mountain pass, in the valleys, and inside the still existing nomadic settlements. Shamshiev, who studied under Alexander Zguridi, was already known for his superb popular-science and documentary films about Kirghizia. The young cameraman Turatbekov showed assurance and talent in the thrilling scene of the nocturnal raid on the herd, the tension, the thud of hooves, hoarse shouts in the semi-darkness; and again, in the scene where the local prince sits at court, where outward calm and splendour conceal ruthless cruelty and the vindictive mockery of man. The film makers were successful, too, with the mass scenes, where the nomads, robbed of all their possessions, are driven from their tribal pastures; and with the lyrical episodes from family life in Bakhtygul's tent.

At present Shamshiev is making an adventure film, *The Curse*, which deals with opium smuggling. Opium poppies have been cultivated in Kirghizia for over fifty years, the morphine being in demand for medicinal use. In the twenties opium was manufactured in Kirghizia by private plantations and farms, and most of it was smuggled abroad. In *The Curse* action centres on the clashes between border guards and smugglers. The famous Polish star Barbara Brylska will appear in the film in the role of an addict.

Modern Uzbek cinema is noteworthy for four significant young men—directors Elier Ishmukhamedov and Ali Khamraev, the scriptwriter Odelsha Agishev and the cameraman Dilshat Fatkhullin. All

* A sect which did not recognise Patriarch Nikon's reforms in the seventeenth century.

Young Soviet Film Makers

Director Bolot Shamshiev on the camera

are VGIK graduates. In 1964 Ishmukhamedov and Fatkhullin made *Rendez-vous*, a short film about two comical students who come to a Kirghiz village for their holidays—the romantic story of city dwellers in the place of their childhood. Ishmukhamedov's next film, *Tenderness* (1966), again with Fatkhullin, attracted much attention during Soviet Film Week in Paris and at the International Film Festival in Locarno especially by its visual originality. The unity of ideas achieved by the three cinéastes Ishmukhamedov, Fatkhullin and Agishev is remarkable. It might have something to do with the fact that their backgrounds are practically identical: childhood in Uzbekistan, studies at the VGIK. *Tenderness* is made with extreme warmth and tender melancholy for their own childhood and adolescence, whose memory must still have been fresh in their minds. It consists of three episodes scripted by Agishev—the first bears the title of the whole film, the other two are named after the heroines *Lena* and *Mamura*. All three episodes are romantic love stories involving young couples. The final scene of *Mamura* is reminiscent of Fellini's *Nights of Cabiria*. Much of the film's mood is contributed by the music: Uzbek, Russian, French, Japanese and Italian songs are sung.

Ishmukhamedov's latest film (again with a script by

The Awakening of the Steppes

The Curse by Bolot Shamshiev

Director Elier Ishmukhamedov directing a scene from *In Love*

O. Agishev) is the feature *In Love* (1969). The trend shown in *Tenderness* and Khutsiev's *I Am Twenty* is further developed. *In Love* is about the youth of today, their destinies and problems. Interwoven, quite freely, are the stories of the love of an ordinary youth for a shallow, selfish girl, and the story of a boy whose father has deserted his home and family. The film manages to create the atmosphere of exotic Bukhara, by extremely good casting, as in the shots of a dancing place full of local long-haired hippies. Couples meet on the dancing floor, fall in love, are jealous, try to imitate what they know about hippy life in the West—just as in real life. The originality of approach, subtleness of allusions, well-executed cutting and music, and uninhibited acting from the young players are characteristic elements of Ishmukhamedov's work. The film is presented in a way destined to evoke controversy, but it is lyrical and reveals an understanding and sympathy for the real life problems of the young. A turbulent river smashing up a barge laden with water-melons, the prolonged dance of the hero who is trying to forget the disappointment and anguish of an unhappy love—these scenes are sheer poetry. The subject is risky and the treatment individualistic, so to placate the censor a rather incongruous insert was added, showing the police beating up a peaceful demonstrator in Greece.

Ali Khamraev made a brilliant feature *White, White Storks* (1966) with the same team—a script by Agishev, and Fatkhullin on camera. The story – unusual for Uzbekistan even today – deals with a married woman who falls in love with another man and decides to marry him in spite of strict traditional taboos and prejudice. Fatkhullin's camerawork is superb—the film seems to absorb the boundless Uzbek steppes, the freshness of unspoilt nature, the texture of clay and wood and images of horses or a foggy sunrise. It was made on location in a large hill village, where the

White, White Storks by Ali Khamraev

The Red Sands by Ali Khamraev

yearly arrival of the storks in the spring is an event for the local inhabitants.

In 1969 Khamraev made a colour film-opera *Dilorom,* after the poems of Alisher Navoi, an Uzbek classical poet and philosopher. *Dilorom* is a tragic story about the love of a slave-girl, Dilorom, and the court painter Moni.

The first Turkmenian film *The Decisive Step* was made from the novel of the Turkmenian writer, Berdy Kerbabaev, and produced by the regional studio in 1966. The Turkmen director Bulat Mansurov graduated from the VGIK in 1963, and made *The Contest* in 1964. The subject is the eternal war between the Turkmen tribes and the Iranian Kurds. The hero, Shukur-bakshi, sees only blood and tears in his land, and fearful that the Khan is gathering troops for a new march, he penetrates the enemy camp in order to participate in a peaceful singing contest. Shukur wins it, and through his dutar-playing tells the assembled company about his wonderful country, thus reversing the ancient dictum, that the Muses fall silent at the clamour of war. The philosophical point of the film is to analyse power and the corruption it brings. The script is interspersed with Saadi's verse, and the whole weight of ancient Asian culture is brought to bear: the Eastern preference for ornamental language and dress, and florid symbols and huge allegorical statements enhance the general impression. The analysis of the unchanging nature of despotism seems to refer as much to the more recent past as to ancient times.

Mansurov's second feature *Quenching the Thirst* (1967) is about the digging of a canal in the Kara-Kum sands. This contemporary subject unfortunately retained the artificial character of the literary original

Young Soviet Film Makers

(a novel by the Soviet writer Y. Trifonov).

In contrast to this, Mansurov had a great success with his recent adaptation of Andrei Platonov's *Takyr, The Slave-Girl* (1970). With dramatic tension and great understanding of his country's past, he has depicted how an old Turkmenian chief, who is childless, buys a Persian slave-girl, who gives him a daughter. The child is regarded as illegitimate by the tribe. In the same village an Austrian former prisoner-of-war and the only European in the area, lives in a deserted tower, where he paints his expressionist visions on the crumbling stone walls. The Austrian is liked by the village children, for whom he stages puppet plays, acting himself in the improvisations as a sad clown. But the villagers distrust him, and when the old Turkmen, Khali-bey, realises that his girl has picked up strange revolutionary ideas from the vagabond, he decides to kill him. The film is very cruel, especially in the sequence when the Austrian, still in his bizarre clown outfit and encircled by a jeering, hostile crowd, desperately tries to avoid the gun pointed at him. There is no doubt that the film owes its great and well deserved success not only to the sensitive work of the director, but also to the skill of the designer S. Akmukhamedov and the cameraman K. Narliev, who contribute so much to the excellent use of colour.

The young Kazakh director, Abdulla Karsakbaev,

Quenching of the Thirst by Bulat Mansurov

The Slave-Girl by Bulat Mansurov

The Awakening of the Steppes

The Slave-Girl by Bulat Mansurov

made a beautiful film *My Name is Kozha* in 1964. An amusing, naughty and boisterous boy, Kozha from a Kazakhstan village is the scourge of the school, of his family and of the neighbours. He reduces his fifth-form schoolmistress to tears and his mother does not know what to do with him. Everyone in the village sympathises with the poor woman. Was his father, a war hero, like that? After a talk with the headmaster the boy promises to himself that he will try to reform and be more like his father. On a school trip to a collective farm to do practical work such as mowing hay and shearing sheep, Kozha thinks 'work is the best way to temper one's will', but his naughtiness takes control again and he does not go. He runs into his 'old pal' Sultan, a good for nothing who had left school long ago and never worked since. Together they go to the mountains to celebrate a festive occasion and they enjoy the trip tremendously. But it all ends sadly for Kozha and only then does the fifth former finally decide to reform and be worthy of his father. The film shows the director's great love for his native Kazakhstan and its village atmosphere.

PART III

10 Appendix I

Soviet Film Studios
There are at present twenty film studios in the Soviet Union which produce feature films. By far the largest of them are the following three studios:

Mosfilm, Moscow
Gorky Film Studio, Moscow
Lenfilm, Leningrad.

The others are:
1. Azerbaidzhanfilm, Baku, Azerbaidzhan SSR
2. Armenfilm, Erevan, Armenian SSR
3. Belarusfilm, Minsk, Belorussian SSR
4. Gruziafilm, Tbilisi, Georgian SSR
5. Kazakhfilm, Alma-Ata, Kazakh SSR
6. Alexander Dovzhenko Kiev Studio, Kiev, Ukrainian SSR
7. Kirghizfilm, Frunze, Kirghiz SSR
8. Moldova-film, Kishinev, Moldavian SSR
9. Lithuanian Film Studio, Vilnius, Lithuanian SSR
10. Odessa Film Studio, Odessa
11. Sverdlovsk Film Studio, Sverdlovsk
12. Tadzhikfilm, Dushanbe, Tadzhik SSR
13. Tallin-Film, Tallin, Estonian SSR
14. Turkmenfilm, Ashkhabad, Turkmen SSR
15. Uzbekfilm, Tashkent, Uzbek SSR
16. Riga Film Studio, Riga, Latvian SSR
17. Yalta Film Studio, Yalta, Crimea

Other film studios are:
VGIK Students' Studio, Moscow
Studio of Popular Science Films, Moscow
Experimental Studio, Moscow
Studio of Popular Science Films, Leningrad
Studio of Popular Science Films, Kiev
Soyuzmultfilm, Moscow
Central Studio of Documentary Films, Moscow
Moscow TV Studio
Leningrad TV Studio
Minsk TV Studio
Tallin TV Studio

Film production (feature films) for all studios from 1958 to 1970 was:
1958 — 116
1959 — 139
1960 — 115
1961 — 125
1962 — 107
1963 — 115
1964 — 102
1965 — 124
1966 — 134
1967 — 130
1968 — 129
1969 — 102
1970 — 134

Appendix I—Soviet Film Studios

Film production (feature films) of the three most important studios from 1958 to 1970 was:

	MOSFILM	LENFILM	GORKY STUDIO
1958	23	17	10
1959	30	16	12
1960	28	18	10
1961	36	16	11
1962	36	16	11
1963	24	11	13
1964	27	10	10
1965	25	13	11
1966	26	12	10
1967	23	19	14
1968	29	14	12
1969	23	11	10
1970	25	15	12

11 Appendix II

Chronological List of Main Films (1956-72)

1956
The Forty First—Grigori Chukhrai
Ignotas Came Back Home—Alexander Razumny
Lurdzha Magdany—Tengiz Abuladze, Rezo Chkheidze
Spring in Zarechnaya Street—Marlen Khutsiev, Felix Mironer
Two Captains—Vladimir Vengerov
1957
The Cranes Are Flying—Mikhail Kalatozov
Otar's Widow—Mikhail Chiaureli
1958
Chieftain Kodr—Mikhail Kalik, Boris Rytsarev
The Girl With the Guitar—Alexander Fainzimmer
Ivan the Terrible (Part II)—Sergei Eisenstein
1959
Adam Wants to Be A Man—Vitautas Zhalakyavichus
Ballad of a Soldier—Grigori Chukhrai
Destiny of a Man—Sergei Bondarchuk
The Letter That Was Not Sent—Mikhail Kalatozov
Living Heroes—Vitautas Zhalakyavichus, Balis Bratkauskas, Marionas Gedris, Arunas Zhebrunas
Two Fyodors—Marlen Khutsiev
1960
From House to House—Otar Abesadze, Merab Kokochashvili
The Lady With a Little Dog—Josef Heifitz
Lullaby—Mikhail Kalik
Splendid Days (Seriozha)—Georgi Danelia, Igor Talankin
The Steam-Roller and the Violin—Andrei Tarkovsky
They Are Also People—Georgi Danelia, Igor Talankin
1961
The Alcohol-makers—Leonid Gaydai
The Amphibian Man—G. Kazansky, V. Chebotaryov
And What If It is Love?—Yuli Raizman
Clear Skies—Grigori Chukhrai
Girls—Yuri Chulukin
Man Following the Sun—Mikhail Kalik
My Friend Kolka—Alexei Saltykov, Alexander Mitta
Nine Days in One Year—Mikhail Romm
Peace to the Newcomer—Alexander Alov, Vladimir Naumov
The Red Sails—Alexander Ptushko
1962
Footsteps in the Night—Raimondas Vabalas
I, Grandma, Iliko and Illarion—Tengiz Abuladze
Ivan's Childhood—Andrei Tarkovsky
Journey into April—Vadim Derbenev
The Way to the Wharf—Georgi Danelia
We, Two Men—Yuri Lysenko
1963
Aunt With Violets—Pavel Lubimov
I Walk About Moscow—Georgi Danelia
Cain 18th—Nadezda Kosheverova, Mikhail Shapiro
Chronicle of One Day—Vitautas Zhalakyavichus

Appendix II—Chronological List of Main Films (1956-71)

The Contest—Bulat Mansurov
Heat—Larissa Shepitko
My Name is Kozha—Abdulla Karsakbaev
Three Plus Two—Georgi Oganesyan
The White Caravan—Eldar Shengelaya, Tamaz Meliava
1964
The Bad Joke—Alexander Alov, Vladimir Naumov
The Chairman—Alexei Saltykov
The Don Story—Vladimir Fetin
Father of A Soldier—Rezo Chkheidze
Hamlet—Grigori Kozintsev
I Am Cuba—Mikhail Kalatozov
I Am Twenty—Marlen Khutsiev
There Was A Lad—Vassili Shukshin
Welcome—Elem Klimov
When Storks Fly Away—Vadim Lysenko
1965
Fidelity—Pyotr Todorovsky
The First Teacher—Andron Mikhalkov-Konchalovsky
Fro—Rezo Esadze
The Girl and the Echo—Arunas Zhebrunas
Hello, It's Me!—Frunze Dovlatyan
I See the Sun—Lana Gogoberidze
Open the Door, When the Bell Rings—Alexander Mitta
Our House—Vassili Pronin
Shadows of Our Forgotten Ancestors—Sergei Paradzhanov
There Was An Old Man and An Old Woman—Grigori Chukhrai
The Thirty Three—Georgi Danelia
The Two—Mikhail Bogin
War And Peace—Sergei Bondarchuk
The Wedding—Mikhail Kobakhidze
1966
Aibolit-66—Rolan Bykov
Andrei Rublev—Andrei Tarkovsky
Asya's Happiness—Andron Mikhalkov-Konchalovsky
Beware the Car!—Eldar Ryazanov
In the Town of S.—Josef Heifitz
Nobody Wanted to Die—Vitautas Zhalakyavichus
Rain in July—Marlen Khutsiev
Red Glades—Emil Lotyanu
Tenderness—Elier Ishmukhamedov
When Leaves Fall—Otar Yoseliani
Wings—Larissa Shepitko
The Women—Pavel Lubimov
Your Son and Brother—Vassili Shukshin
1967
The Adventures of A Dentist—Elem Klimov
Anna Karenina—Alexander Zarkhi
Bitter Grains—Valeri Gazhiu, Vadim Lysenko
The Captive Girl of the Caucasus—Leonid Gaydai
Four Pages of A Young Life—Rezo Esadze
Hurrying on the Waves—Pavel Lubimov
The Kingdom of Women—Alexei Saltykov
Lelka—Pavel Arsenov
The Little Prince—Arunas Zhebrunas
Matsy Khvitia (He Did Not Want to Kill)—Georgi Shengelaya
Quenching of the Thirst—Bulat Mansurov
Sky of Our Childhood—Tolomush Okeev
The Umbrella—Mikhail Kobakhidze
White, White Storks—Ali Khamraev
Wide Green Valley—Merab Kokochashvili
Zosya—Mikhail Bogin
1968
The Appeal—Tengiz Abuladze
The Enigmatic Indian—Pyotr Todorovsky
No Ford In the Fire—Gleb Panfilov
On the Eve of Ivan Kupala Day—Yuri Ilyenko
Three Days of Victor Chernyshev—Mark Osepyan
1969
The Beautiful Girl—Arunas Zhebrunas

Young Soviet Film Makers

Cheer Up!—Georgi Danelia
The Diamond Arm—Leonid Gaydai
The Director—Alexei Saltykov
Gunshot at the Mountain Pass—Bolot Shamshiev
In Love—Elier Ishmukhamedov
A Nest of Gentlefolk—Andron Mikhalkov-Konchalovsky
The New Girl—Pavel Lubimov
The Red Sands—Ali Khamraev, K. Akbarkhodzhaev
The Slave-Girl—Bulat Mansurov
Spring Will Come Soon—Otar Abesadze
Ten Winters In One Summer—Valeri Gazhiu
This Moment—Emil Lotyanu
Virineya—Vladimir Fetin
When I Was Young—Algirdas Araminas
1970
The Ballerina—Vadim Derbenev
Colour of the Pomegranate (Sayat Nova)—Sergei Paradzhanov
A Day Ahead—Pavel Lubimov
Death of A Philatelist—Georgi Kalatozishvili
The Debut—Gleb Panfilov
Heritage—Tolomush Okeev
The King-Deer—Pavel Arsenov
King Lear—Grigori Kozintsev
Love, Dagger and Treason—Eldar Shengelaya
Lubov Yarovaya—Vladimir Fetin
The Musicians—Mikhail Kobakhidze

Shine, O, Shine, My Star!—Alexander Mitta
Strange People—Vassili Shukshin
Tchaikovsky—Igor Talankin
Uncle Vanya—Andron Mikhalkov-Konchalovsky
Waterloo—Sergei Bondarchuk
1971
About Love—Mikhail Bogin
Day After Day—Otar Yoseliani
The Leutary—Emil Lotyanu
Merry-Go-Round—Mikhail Shveitser
Pirosmani—Georgi Shengelaya
The Seagull—Yuli Karasik
Flight—Alexander Alov, Vladimir Naumov
Sport, Sport, Sport—Elem Klimov
White Bird With a Black Spot—Yuri Ilyenko
You And Me—Larissa Shepitko
Andrei Rublev—Andrei Tarkovsky (release—December 1971)
1972
Solaris—Andrei Tarkovsky
Zakhar Berkut—Leonid Osyka
Jeanne d'Arc—Gleb Panfilov
I am a Detective—George Kalatozishvili
Battle of Berlin—Yuri Ozerov
A Drama of Former Times—Ilya Averbakh
The Telegram—Rolan Bykov
The Star of my Town—Otar Abesadze

12 Filmographies

Otar Abesadze
b. 1939 in Georgia. Graduated from the VGIK as a director.
Short films
The Reed (1960)
From House To House (1960)
Prod. Gruzia-Film; dir. O. Abesadze, M. Kokochashvili; sc. R. Tabukashvili; ph. A. Filipashvili; des. Z. Medzmariashvili, T. Krymkovskaya; mus. A. Kereselidze; players: G. Talakvadze, S. Takaishvili, G. Tkabladze, K. Abesadze, N. Chkheidze, M. Medzmariashvili, G. Mdivani.
Feature films
The Spring Will Come Soon (1969)
Prod. Gruzia-Film; dir. O. Abesadze; sc. O. Yoseliani, T. Maglaperidze; ph. A. Maysuradze; players: S. Zakariadze, S. Takayshvili, T. Archvadze, N. Machavariani, L. Eliava.

Odelsha Agishev
b. 1939 in Tataria. Graduated from the Suvorov Military College, then from the VGIK as a scriptwriter (1963).
Scripts
Storm Over Asia (1964, in collaboration with K. Yarmatov); *Tenderness* (1966); *The White, White Storks* (1966); *In Love* (1969); *The Cheka Commissar* (1970).

Algirdas Araminas
b. 1937 in Lithuania. Graduated from the VGIK as a cameraman.
Shot
Nightingale (1959) (one episode from *Living Heroes*); *Strangers* (1962); *The Chronicle of One Day* (1963).
Feature films
The Nights Without Lodging (1967)
Prod. Lithuanian Film Studio (Vilnius); dir. A. Araminas, G. Karka; sc. V. Ognev; ph. D. Pechura; players: S. Petronaytis, E. Matulayte, R. Zdanavichute, D. Melenayte, A. Masulis, Y. Miltinis, K. Vitkus, B. Barauskas.
Find Me (1968)
Prod. Lithuanian Film Studio; dir. A. Araminas; sc. G. Kanovichus, V. Rimkyavichus; ph. D. Pechura; players: E. Pleshkite, Y. Urmanavichus, V. Lizdenite.
When I Was Young (1969) after Matti Unt's story *Red Cat, Good-bye!* Prod. Lithuanian Film Studio; dir. A. Araminas; sc. I. Meras, A. Araminas; ph. D. Pechura; des. A. Nichus; mus. A. Apyanavichus; players: L. Krischunas, Y. Kavalyauskayte.

Pavel Arsenov
b. 1940 in Tbilisi (Georgia). Graduated from the VGIK as a director (1962).
Short films
Sunflower (1963)

Young Soviet Film Makers

Prod. Gorky Studios; dir. P. Arsenov; sc. V. Zakrutkin; ph. P. Kataev; des. M. Gorelik; mus. I. Kataev; players: V. Maliavina, P. Shpringfeld, I. Kuznetsov, V. Minin, N. Smirnov.
Lelka (1967) (one episode from *The Awakening*). Prod. Gorky Studios; dir. P. Arsenov; sc. Y. Yakovlev; ph. V. Kornilov; players: L. Nerchenko, D. Scherbakov, N. Smirnov.
Rescue A Drowning Man (1968)
Prod. Gorky Studios; dir. P. Arsenov; sc. A. Zak, I. Kuznetsov; ph. G. Garibyan; players: A. Ushakov, L. Karasev.
King-Deer (1970)
Prod. Gorky Studios; dir. P. Arsenov; sc. V. Korostylev; ph. I. Zarafyan; des. A. Boim; mus. M. Tariverdiev; players: Y. Yakovlev, V. Maliavina, S. Ursky, V. Shlezinger, E. Solovey, V. Zozulin, O. Tabakov, O. Efremov.

Mikhail Bogin
b. 1936 in Leningrad. Two years at the Leningrad Polytechnical Institute. Graduated from the VGIK as a director. Assistant director to Joseph Heifitz on *The Lady With a Little Dog*.
Short films
Ten Seconds in an Hour (documentary, stud. work)
The Two (1965)
Prod. Riga Film Studio; dir. M. Bogin; sc. M. Bogin, Y. Chulukin; ph. R. Pik, G. Pilipson; des. T. Antonova; mus. Grinblat; players: V. Fyodorova, V. Smirnitsky.
Feature films
Zosya (1967)
Prod. Gorky Studios; dir. M. Bogin; sc. V. Bogomolov; ph. J. Lipman; des. R. Wolyniec; mus. R. Khozak; players: Pola Raksa, Y. Kamorny, N. Merzlikhin, V. Mazurkevitch, Z. Tzintel, B. Bargelovska, A. Grave, G. Burkov, N. Khangazhiev.
About Love (1971)
Prod. Gorky Studios; dir. M. Bogin; sc. M. Bogin, Y. Klepikov; ph. C. Filippov; des. M. Gorelik, A. Valerianov; mus. E. Krylatov; players: V. Fyodorova, S. Dreyen, E. Shashkova, V. Tikhonov, O. Yankovsky, V. Gaft, B. Anderson.

Georgi Danelia
b. 1930 in Georgia. Architect. Graduated from the two year directors' course at Mosfilm Studios (1960).
Short film
They Are Also People (1959, co-directed with I. Talankin)
Feature films
Seryozha (*The Splendid Days*, 1960) with I. Talankin
Prod. Mosfilm; dir. G. Danelia, I. Talankin; sc. V. Panova, G. Danelia, I. Talankin; ph. A. Nitochkin; des. V. Nisskaya; mus. B. Tchaikovsky; players: B. Barkhatov, S. Bondarchuk, I. Skobtseva.
The Way to the Wharf (1962)
Prod. Mosfilm; dir. G. Danelia; sc. V. Konetsky; ph. A. Nitochkin; des. A. Borisov; mus. A. Petrov; players: B. Andreev, O. Zhakov, L. Sokolova, A. Metelkin, V. Nikulin, Oya Bruno.
I Walk About Moscow (1963)
Prod. Mosfilm; dir. G. Danelia; sc. G. Shpalikov; ph. V. Yusov; players: Y. Leonov, N. Mordiukova, I. A. Loktev, N. Mikhalkov, G. Polskikh, Y. Steblov.
The Thirty Three (1965)
Prod. Mosfilm; dir. G. Danelia; sc. V. Konetsky; ph. V. Yusov; players: Y. Leonov, N. Mordiukova, I. Churikova.
Cheer Up! (1969)
Prod. Gruzia Film; dir. G. Danelia; sc. R. Gabriadze; ph. V. Yusov; des. D. Takayshvili; mus. G. Kangeli; players: Buba Kikabidze, S. Zakariadze, A. Vertins-

kaya, S. Filippov, G. Kavtaradze, S. Chiaureli, Y. Leonov.

Vadim Derbenev
b. 1934. Graduated from the VGIK as cameraman (1957).
Shot
Chieftain Kodr (1959); *Lullaby* (1960); *Man Following the Sun* (1961); *Horizon* (1961).
Feature films
Journey into April (1963)
Prod. Moldova Film Studio; dir. and ph. V. Derbenev; ph. (asst.) D. Motorny; sc. D. Vasiliu, L. Rutitsky, A. Busujok; des. A. Mater; mus. E. Lazarev; players: A. Zbruev, R. Nedashkovskaya, T. Gruzin, J. Zotsenko, Y. Floria, V. Vasiliev.
The Last Month of the Autumn (1965)
Prod. Moldova Film Studio; dir. and ph. V. Derbenev; sc. J. Druttze; ph. (asst.) D. Motorny; des. A. Mater; mus. E. Lazarev; players: E. Lebedev, V. Sperantova, N. Timofeev, M. Bulgakova.
The Knight of the Dream (1969)
Prod. Moldova Film Studio; dir. and sc. and ph. V. Derbenev with L. Rutitsky (sc.); players: E. Ushakov, N. Simonov, M. Kushnirova, A. Lazarev, F. Nikitin.
Ballerina (1970)
Prod. Mosfilm; dir. and sc. and ph. V. Derbenev; des. L. Shengelia; mus. M. Chulaki, R. Schedrin; players: Maya Plisetskaya, N. Fadeechev.

Rezo Esadze
b. 1935 in Georgia. Graduated Tbilisi University as physicist-mathematician, and later from the VGIK as a director.
Short films
One Day (1963, stud. work)

Fro (1965)
Prod. Lenfilm; dir. R. Esadze; sc. F. Mironer; ph. K. Sobolev, V. Fyodorov; des. V. Zatchiniaev; mus. I. Shvartz; players: A. Zavyalova, N. Trofimov, A. Freyndlikh.
Feature films
Four Pages from a Young Life (1967)
Prod. Lenfilm; dir. R. Esadze; sc. V. Panova; ph. E. Yakovlev; des. A. Rudyakov; mus. I. Schvartz; players: B. Rudnev, N. Velichko, A. Zavyalova.
Stopwatch (1970)
Prod. Lenfilm; dir. R. Esadze; sc. L. Zorin; ph. V. Fedosov; des. B. Bykov; mus. O. Karavaychuk; players: S. Olyalin, L. Oleshnikova, N. Antonova, V. Beskova.

Vladimir Fetin
b. 1936. Graduated from the VGIK (G. Kozintsev's pupil) in 1959.
Short films
The Secret of Youth (1956); *The First Car* (1957); *And How Are You?* (1958)
The Foal (1959)
Prod. Lenfilm; dir. V. Fetin; sc. A. Vitol (after Sholokhov's story); ph. E. Kirpichev; des. A. Rudyakov; mus. V. Solovyev-Sedoy; players: E. Matveev, L. Parkhomenko, C. Polezhaev.
Feature films
The Striped Load (1961)
Prod. Lenfilm; dir. V. Fetin; sc. A. Kapler, V. Konetzky; ph. D. Meskhiev; des. A. Rudyakov; mus. V. Basner; players: A. Grobov, I. Dmitriev, M. Makarova, Y. Leonov, V. Belokurov, N. Volkov.
The Don Story (1964)
Prod. Lenfilm; dir. V. Fetin; sc. A. Vitol; ph. Y. Kirpichev; des. A. Rudyakov; mus. V. Soloviev-Sedoy; players: Y. Leonov, L. Chursina, A. Blinov,

Young Soviet Film Makers

B. Novikov, N. Melnikov.
Virineya (1969)
Prod. Lenfilm; dir. V. Fetin; sc. A. Shulgina; ph. Y. Shapiro; des. L. Shiliva; mus. V. Soloviev-Sedoy; players: L. Chursina, A. Papanov, V. Nevinny, V. Vladimirova, N. Fedosova, V. Chalevich, Y. Leonov, O. Borisov, A. Trusov.
Lubov Yarovaya (1970)
Prod. Lenfilm; dir. V. Fetin; sc. A. Vitol; ph. Y. Shapiro; des. I. Vuskovich; mus. V. Soloviev-Sedoy; players: L. Chursina, V. Lanovoy, R. Nifontova, V. Shukshin, K. Lavrov, A. Papanov, N. Alisova.

Rezo Gabriadze
b. 1939 in Kutaisi (Georgia). Graduated at the Higher Scriptwriters' Courses in Moscow. Was correspondent on the Youth of Georgia newspaper.
Scripts
An Unusual Exhibition; Cheer Up!; Feola; The Pitcher; Serenade; Love, Dagger and Treason.

Valeri Gazhiu
b. 1938 in Moldavia. Graduated from the VGIK as a scriptwriter.
Scripts
Man Following the Sun (1961); *When Storks Fly Away* (1964).
Short Film (as director and scriptwriter)
The Street Listens (1964).
Feature films
Bitter Grains (1967)
Prod. Moldova Film Studio; dir. and sc. V. Gazhiu, V. Lysenko; ph. V. Kalashnikov; players: I. Shkurya, L. Nevedomsky, Y. Gorobetz, M. Helaste-Garshnek.
Ten Winters In One Summer (1969)
Prod. Moldova Film Studio; dir. and sc. V. Gazhiu, V. Yegorov (co-sc.); ph. L. Proskurov; des. S. Bulgakov, A. Roman; mus. V. Dova; players: K. Konstantinov, G. Grigoriu, Z. Tzakhilova, M. Volontir.
Time Bomb (1971)
Prod. Moldova Film Studio; dir. V. Gazhiu; sc. M. Melnik, B. Saakov, V. Gazhiu; ph. L. Proskurov; des. V. Kobrig, N. Apostolidze; mus. E. Doga; players: A. Azo, S. Sokolovsky, L. Malevanaya.

Marionas Vintzo Gedris
b. 1933 in Lithuania. Graduated from the VGIK as a director.
Short films
The Sky Belongs to Us (1964); *The Anniversary* (1965); *The Song About Flax* (1965); *Do-Re-Mi* (1966); *The Hen and Horses* (1966).
We Do Not Need Anyone Now (1960) (one episode of *Living Heroes*)
Prod. Lithuanian Film Studio; dir. and sc. M. Gedris; ph. D. Pechura, R. Verba; des. M. Bulaka, A. Zhebrunas; mus. Y. Balsis; players: N. Narkis, K. Vitkus.
The Strangers (1962).
The Summer of Men (1970)
Prod. Lithuanian Film Studio; dir. M. Gedris; sc. A. Yurovsky, S. Shaltyanis; ph. A. Motskus; des. A. Nichus; mus. V. Iozapaytis; players: R. Adomaitis, I. Budraitis, A. Shurno.

Yevgeni Grigoriev
b. 1937 in Grozny (North Caucasus) Was a builder-worker. Graduated from the VGIK as a scriptwriter.
Scripts
Our House (1965) *Three Days of Victor Chernyshev* (1968).

Yuri Ilyenko

b. 1936. Graduated from the VGIK as cameraman (1960)
Shot
Goodbye, Doves (1960); *Somewhere There is a Son* (1962); *Shadows of Our Forgotten Ancestors* (1965).
Acted
1, Newton Street (1963).
Feature films (as director and cameraman)
On the Eve of Ivan Kupala Day (1968)
Prod. Dovzhenko Kiev Studio; dir. and ph. Y. Ilyenko; sc. Drach; players: L. Kadochnikova, B. Khmelnitsky.
White Bird With a Black Spot (1971).

Elier Ishmukhamedov

b. 1942 in Uzbekistan. Graduated from the VGIK as a director.
Short film
Rendez-vous (1963)
Prod. Uzbekfilm Studio; dir. E. Ishmukhamedov; sc. Ishmukhamedov, Fatkhullin; ph. D. Fatkhullin; des. H. Bakaev; mus. R. Vildanov; players: U. Khodzhaev, B. Ikhtiarov, M. Arifudzhanova.
Feature films
Tenderness (1966)
Prod. Uzbekfilm Studio; dir. Ishmukhamedov; sc. O. Agishev; ph. D. Fatkhullin; des. M. Chochiev, S. Ziyamukhamedov; mus. V. Trotszuk; players: M. Sternikova, R. Nakhapetov, R. Sagdulaev, R. Agzamov, M. Makhmudova.
In Love (1969)
Prod. Uzbekfilm Studio; dir. Ishmukhamedov; sc. O. Agishev; ph. G. Tutunov; des. M. Chochiev, S. Ziyamukhamedov; mus. V. Trotszuk; players: A. Vertinskaya, R. Nakhapetov, R. Sagdulaev.

Georgi Kalatozishvili

b. 1937 in Georgia. Graduated from the VGIK as a cameraman.
Shot
I, Grandma, Iliko And Illarion (1962); *The White Caravan* (1963); *I See The Sun* (1965); *He Did Not Want To Kill* (1967).
Feature film
Death of a Philatelist (1970)
Prod. Gruzia Film Studios; dir. and sc. G. Kalatozishvili with L. Alexidze and A. Salukvadze; ph. Y. Kikabidze; des. D. Takayshvili; mus. K. Pevzner; players: R. Chkhekvadze, R. Kiknadze, A. Kurdiani, V. Sulakvelidze.

Gela Kandelaki

b. 1940 in Georgia. Graduated from the VGIK as a director (1969).
Short films
Red Square (1964); *Quiet, Long Melody* (documentary, 1966).
Feature film
Today (1965)
Prod. VGIK studio; dir. and sc. G. Kandelaki (stud. work).

Abdulla Karsakbaev

b. 1940 in Kazakhstan. Graduated from the VGIK as a director.
Feature films
My Name Is Kozha (1964)
Prod. Kazakhfilm Studios; dir. A. Karsakbaev; sc. B. Sokpakbaev, N. Zeleransky; ph. A. Kasteev; des. I. Karsakbaev; players: B. Rimova, R. Mukhamedyarova, K. Kozabekov.
The Anxious Morning (1968)
Prod. Kazakhfilm Studios; dir. A. Karsakbaev; sc. E.

Shashkin, O. Suleymenova; ph. A. Kasteev; des. I. Karsakbaev; players: I. Nogaybaev, E. Popov, A. Ashimov, A. Shamicv.
Journey into Childhood (1970)
Prod. Kazakhfilm Studios; dir. A. Karsakbaev; sc. B. Sokpakbaev, L. Tolstoy; ph. M. Aranyshev; des. I. Karsakbaev; mus. N. Tlendiev; players: N. Ikhtimbaev, M. Kulambaev, K. Zhakibaev, R. Mukhamedyarova-Musrepova.

Ali Khamraev
b. 1937 in Uzbekistan. Graduated from the VGIK as a director.
Short film
Salom, Bakhor (1963).
Feature films
In the Sunshine (1958); *The Story Of Mirab* (1959).
Short Stories About Children, Which . . . (1961)
Prod. Tadjikfilm Studio; dir. A. Khamraev, M. Makhmudov; sc. E. Smirnova; ph. P. Terpsikhorov; des. Y. Kladienko, R. Muradyan; mus. F. Saliev, Y. Ter-Osipov; players: R. Alimov, K. Mansurov, F. Bobokalonova, S. Amrutdinov.
She Loves Me, She Loves Me Not . . . (1964)
Prod. Tadjikfilm; dir. A. Khamraev; sc. M. Rabiev, M. Melkumov, V. Mass, M. Chervinsky; ph. B. Serdin; des. G. Yungvald-Khilkevich; mus. A. Zatszepin; players: C. Azamatova, B. Jurabaev, M. Aripov, S. Borodina, A. Kasymov, A. Latfi, M. Yakubova.
Where Are You, My Zulfija? (1964)
Prod. Uzbekfilm; dir. A. Khamraev; sc. O. Agishev, A. Khamraev; ph. D. Fatkhullin; des. S. Abdusalamov; mus. R. Vildanov; players: B. Beyshenaliev, S. Isaeva, M. Rafikov, K. Latinov.
White, White Storks (1967);
The Red Sands (1969)
Prod. Uzbekfilm; dir. A. Khamraev, K. Akbarkhodzhaev; sc. K. Ikramov, A. Makarov; ph. A. Pak; des. A. Shibaev; mus. R. Vildanov; players: B. Beyshenaliev, A. Jalyev, A. Azo, G. Ismaylova, K. Umarov, D. Oraev.
Dilorom (1969)
Prod. Uzbekfilm; dir. A. Khamraev; sc. K. Yashen, A. Khamraev; ph. H. Fayziev; des. E. Kalantarov; mus. M. Ashrafi; players: G. Khamraeva, S. Irgashev.
The Cheka Commissar (1970)
Prod. Uzbekfilm; dir. A. Khamraev; sc. O. Agishev, A. Khamraev; ph. K. Fayziev; des. E. Kalantarov; players: S. Chokmorov, A. Dzhigarkhanyan.

Elem Klimov
b. 1935. Graduated as aviation engineer. Later, as a director from the VGIK.
Short films
The Suitor (silent, stud. work); *Careful Banality!* (stud. work); *Look—the Sky!* (stud. work).
Feature films
Welcome (1964)
Prod. Mosfilm; dir. E. Klimov; sc. S. Lungin, I. Nusinov; ph. A. Kuznetsov; des. V. Kamsky, B. Blank; mus. M. Tariverdiev; players: Y. Yevstigneev, A. Aleynikova, I. Rutberg, L. Smirnova, V. Kosykh.
Adventures of a Dentist (1967)
Prod. Mosfilm; dir. E. Klimov; sc. A. Volodin; ph. S. Rubashkin; des. B. Blank, V. Kamsky; mus. A. Shnitke; players: A. Myagkov, B. Vasilyeva, A. Freyndlikh, P. Krymov, I. Kvasha.
Sport, Sport, Sport (1971)
Prod. Mosfilm; dir. E. Klimov; sc. H. Klimov; ph. B. Brozhovsky, O. Zguridi; des. N. Serebryakov, A. Speshneva; mus. A. Shnitke; players: G. Svetlani, L. Novozhilova, B. Andreev, V. Lyakhov, V. Brumel, H. Klimov, N. Mikhalkov, L. Shepitko.

Filmographies

Mikhail Kobakhidze
b. 1939 in Georgia. Graduated from the VGIK as a director (1965).
Short films
The Merry-Go-Round (1962, stud. work);
Young Love (1964, stud. work);
The Wedding (1965)
Prod. Gruzia-Film; dir. and sc. and mus. arran. M. Kobakhidze; ph. G. Sukhishvili; des. G. Gigauri; players: G. Kavtaradze, N. Kavtaradze.
The Umbrella (1967)
Prod. Gruzia-Film; dir. and sc. and mus. arr. M. Kobakhidze; ph. G. Sukhishvili.
The Musicians (1970)
Prod. Gruzia-Film, dir. and sc. and mus. arr. M. Kobakhidze; ph. G. Sukhishvili.

Merab Kokochashvili
b. 1935 in Georgia. Graduated from the VGIK as a director.
Short films
The Old Beech (1957, stud. work); *From House To House* (1960) with O. Abesadze;
Mikha (1964) (one episode from *Pages of the Past*)
Prod. Gruzia-Film; dir. and sc. M. Kokochashvili; ph. G. Gersamia; des. V. Arabidze; mus. N. Mamisashvili; players: M. Chubinidze, M. Bakhtadze.
Feature films
The School Holidays (1963)
Prod. Gruzia-Film; dir. M. Kokochashvili; sc. R. Inanishvili; ph. A. Filipashvili; des. V. Arabidze, A. Veruishvili; mus. I. Gedmadze; players: G. Gegechkori, M. Kokochashvili, O. Argutashvili, M. Mandzhalagadze.
The Wide Green Valley (1967)
Prod. Gruzia-Film; dir. M. Kokochashvili; sc. M. Eliozishvili; ph. G. Gersamia.

Emil Lotyanu
b. 1937 in Moldavia. Graduated from the VGIK as a director.
Short film
There Was a Boy (1960)
Prod. Moldova-Film; dir. and sc. E. Lotyanu; ph. N. Kharin; des. F. Khemaruru; mus. Z. Tkach; players: A. Basalin, A. Kramarchuk, I. Levianu, A. Yakishin.
Feature films
Wait For Us At Dawn (1963)
Prod. Moldova-Film; dir. and sc. E. Lotyanu, I. Prut (co-sc.); ph. L. Proskurov; des. S. Bulgakov, A. Roman; mus. G. Niaga, V. Syrokhvatov; players: I. Guzhu, V. Panarin, I. Shkurya, D. Karachobanu, V. Volchik.
The Red Glades (1966)
Prod. Moldova-Film; dir. and sc. E. Lotyanu; ph. V. Chiurya, I. Bolbochunu; players: S. Toma, V. Voynichesku, G. Grigoriu.
This Moment (1969)
Prod. Moldova-Film; dir. and sc. E. Lotyanu; ph. V. Churya; des. L. Fernandes, E. Rodriges; players: M. Sotzky-Voynichesku, S. Toma, M. Sagaydak, K. Fernandes, H. Luis Gomes.
The Leutary (1971)
Prod. Moldova-Film; dir. E. Lotyanu; players: D. Khebeshesku, O. Kyapianu, V. Musayan.

Pavel Lubimov
b. 1938 in Moscow. Graduated from the VGIK as a director. Assistant director to S. Rostotsky on *In The Seven Winds* (1962).
Short film
The Aunt With Violets (1963)
Prod. Gorky Studios; dir. P. Lubimov; sc. A. Grebnev; ph. M. Yakovich, M. Osepyan; des. P. Pashkevich; mus. P. Chekalov; players: N. Sazonova,

S. Svetlichnaya, V. Ivashov.
Feature films
The Women (1966)
Prod. Gorky Studios; dir. P. Lubimov; sc. B. Metalnikov; ph. V. Dultzev, M. Osepyan; des. A. Klopotovsky; mus. Y. Frenkel; players: I. Makarova, N. Sazonova, N. Fedosova, G. Yatzkina.
Hurrying on the Waves (1967)
Prod. Gorky Studios and Sofia Studio (Bulgaria); dir. P. Lubimov; sc. A. Galich, S. Tzanev; ph. S. Zlychkin; des. A. Denkov, G. Anfilova; mus. Y. Frenkel; players: N. Bogunova, S. Khashimov, R. Bykov.
The New Girl (1969)
Prod. Gorky Studios; dir. P. Lubimov; sc. P. Lubimov, S. Tokarev; ph. S. Filippov; des. A. Vagichev, N. Kirukhina; mus. Y. Frenkel; players: I. Eliseeva, N. Filippov, I. Makarova, Z. Slavina, V. Gaft, E. Kolmykova, N. Sazonova.
A Day Ahead (1970)
Prod. Gorky Studios; dir. P. Lubimov; sc. I. Velembovskaya; ph. S. Filippov; des. S. Serebrenikov; mus. Y. Frenkel; players: M. Bulgakova, N. Fedosova, L. Nevedomsky, V. Solomin.

Vadim Lysenko
b. 1937 in Moldavia. Graduated from the VGIK as a director.
Feature films
At the Outskirts (1961)
Prod. Moldova-Film; dir. V. Lysenko; sc. Y. Edlis, V. Lysenko; ph. L. Proskurov; des. A. Mater; mus. D. Fedov; players: L. Butenina, B. Shalevich, V. Emelyanov, D. Darienko, M. Gavrilko, V. Zakharchenko, V. Uralsky.
When The Storks Fly Away (1964)
Prod. Moldova-Film; dir. V. Lysenko; sc. V. Gazhiu; ph. V. Kalashnikov; players: N. Mordvinov.
Bitter Grains (1967) with V. Gazhiu (see V. Gazhiu).

Bulat Mansurov
b. 1937 in Turkmenistan. Graduated from the VGIK as a director.
Feature films
The Contest (1963)
Prod. Turkmenfilm; dir. and sc. B. Mansurov; ph. K. Narliev; des. E. Kordysh; mus. N. Khalmamedov; players: A. Khanduryev, A. Dyhalyev, K. Overgelenov, Y. Beknazarov.
Quenching of the Thirst (1967)
Prod. Turkmenfilm; dir. and sc. B. Mansurov, Y. Trifonov (sc); ph. K. Narliev; des. V. Artykov; mus. R. Redzhepov; players: P. Aleynikov, K. Naliev, A. Dzhalyev, L. Satanovsky, O. Zhakov, T. Aleynikov, R. Nedashkovskaya.
The Slave-Girl (1969)
Prod. Turkmenfilm; dir. and sc. B. Mansurov; ph. K. Narliev; des. K. Akmukhamedov; mus. R. Redzhebov; players: T. Aleynikov, N. Geldyeva, G. Nurdisanova, B. Apapov.
There is No Death, Boys! (1970)
Prod. Turkmenfilm; dir. B. Mansurov; sc. S. Ataev; ph. V. Kalashnikov; des. G. Brusentzev; mus. N. Bogoslovsky; players: A. Dzhaliev, H. Akhmukhamedov, Y. Zharikov.

Tamaz Meliava
b. 1929 in Georgia. Graduated from the VGIK as a director (1959).
Feature films
At the Quiet Pier (1959); *White Caravan* (1964, with E. Shengelaya); *Londre* (1966).

Andron Mikhalkov-Konchalovsky

b. 1937 in Moscow. Began training at Moscow Conservatoire as pianist, later graduated from the VGIK as a director. Wrote many scripts: *The Steam-Roller and the Violin* (1961); *Andrei Rublev* (1964 with A. Tarkovsky); *Tashkent – The Bread City* (1969); *The Song of Manshuk* (1969); *The End of the Chieftain* (1970).

Short film
The Boy and the Pigeon (1961)
Feature films
The First Teacher (1965)
Prod. Mosfilm and Kirghizfilm; dir. Mikhalkov-Konchalovsky; sc. Ch. Aytmatov, B. Dobrodeev, Mikhalkov-Konchalovsky; ph. G. Rerberg; des. M. Romadin; mus. V. Ovchinnikov; players: B. Beyshenaliev, N. Arinbasarova.
Asya's Happiness (1966)
Prod. Mosfilm; dir. A. Mikhalkov-Konchalovsky; sc. Y. Klepikov; des. M. Romadin; mus. V. Ovchinnikov; players: Iya Savina.
A Nest of Gentlefolk (1969)
Prod. Mosfilm; dir. A. Mikhalkov-Konchalovsky; sc. V. Yezhov, A. Mikhalkov-Konchalovsky; ph. G. Rerberg; des. A. Boym, N. Dvigubsky, M. Romadin; mus. V. Ovchinnikov; players: L. Kulagin, I. Kupchenko, N. Mikhalkov, B. Tyszkiewicz.
Uncle Vanya (1970)
Prod. Mosfilm; dir. A. Mikhalkov-Konchalovsky; sc. A. Mikhalkov-Konchalovsky; ph. G. Rerberg; des. N. Dvigubsky; mus. A. Shnitke; players: S. Bondarchuk, I. Smoktunovsky, I. Kupchenko, I. Miroshnichenko.

Alexander Mitta

b. 1933. Graduated Building Construction Institute. Worked as cartoonist for humour magazine *Krocodil*. Later, graduated from the VGIK as a director (1961).

Feature films
My Friend Kolka (1961, with Alexei Saltykov) Prod. Mosfilm; dir. A. Mitta, A. Saltykov; sc. A. Khmelik, S. Yermolinsky; ph. V. Maslenikov; des. A. Zharenov; mus. L. Shvartz; players: S. Kobozes, A. Rodionova, A. Dmitrieva, A. Kuznetsov.
Without Fear or Reproach (1963)
Prod. Mosfilm; dir. A. Mitta; sc. S. Lungin, I. Nusinov; ph. G. Shatrov; des. V. Gladnikov; mus. N. Bogoslovsky; players: A. Vitruk, V. Glazkov, N. Burlyaev, S. Kramarov, M. Strizhenova, H. Maksimova.
Open the Door When the Bell Rings (1966) Prod. Mosfilm; dir. A. Mitta; sc. A. Volodin; ph. A. Panasuk; des. P. Kiselev; mus. V. Basner; players: R. Bykov, H. Proklova, V. Kosykh, V. Sysoev.
Shine, O! Shine, My Star! (*The Comedy About Iskremas*) (1970) Prod. Mosfilm; dir. A. Mitta; sc. Y. Dunsky, V. Frid; ph. Y. Sokol; des. B. Blank; mus. B. Tchaikovsky; players: O. Tabakov, H. Proklova, L. Kuravlev, Y. Leonov, O. Yefremov, L. Sokolova.

Tolomush Okeev

b. 1934 in Kirghizia. Graduated at Leningrad Film Institute of Cinema Engineers. Then, the two years directors' course at Mosfilm Studios (1964).

Short films
There Are Horses (1965); *Boom* (1968); *Mountain Necklace* (1969).
Feature films
The Sky of Our Childhood (1967)
Prod. Kirghizfilm; dir. T. Okeev; sc. O. Omurkulov, T. Okeev; ph. K. Kydyraliev; des. S. Ishenov; mus. T. Ermatov; players: M. Ryskulov.
The Heritage (1970)
Prod. Kirghizfilm; dir. T. Okeev.

Young Soviet Film Makers

Mark Osepyan
b. 1937 in Moscow. Graduated at the director's course of the Mosfilm Studio as a cameraman.
Shot
Vienna's Forest (1962); *The Aunt With Violets* (1963); *The Women* (1966).
Feature film
Three Days of Victor Chernyshev (1968)
Prod. Gorky Studios; dir. M. Osepyan; sc. Y. Grigoriev; ph. M. Yakovich; des. V. Dulenkov; mus. A. Rybnikov; players: G. Korolkov, V. Vladimirova, A. Chernov, L. Prygunov, G. Sayfulin, V. Belyakov.

Gleb Panfilov
b. 1933 in Sverdlovsk, chemical engineer. Graduated at the two year directors' course at Mosfilm Studios.
Feature films
No Ford in the Fire (1968)
Prod. Lenfilm; dir. G. Panfilov; sc. G. Panfilov, Y. Gabrilovich; ph. D. Dolinin; players: I. Churikova, M. Bulgakova, M. Kononov, A. Solonitzin.
The Debut (1970)
Prod. Lenfilm; dir. G. Panfilov; sc. G. Panfilov, Y. Gabrilovich; ph. D. Dolinin; des. M. Gaukhman-Sverdlov; mus. V. Bibergan; players: I. Churikova, L. Kuravlev, M. Kononov, N. Skomorokhova, T. Bedova, Y. Klepikov, G. Belov.

Alexei Saltykov
b. 1934. Graduated from the VGIK as a director (M. Romm's class).
Feature films
My friend Kolka (1961, with A. Mitta) see A. Mitta.
Beat The Drum (1962)
Prod. Mosfilm; dir. A. Saltykov; sc. S. Ermolinsky, A. Khmelik; ph. G. Tzekavy, V. Yakushev; des. A. Berger; mus. N. Karetnikov; players: A. Krychenkov,

L. Slepneva, A. Demyanenko, S. Kramarov, V. Ovanesov.
The Chairman (1964)
Prod. Mosfilm; dir. A. Saltykov; sc. Y. Nagibin; ph. V. Nikolaev; des. S. Ushakov; mus. A. Kholminov; players: M. Ulyanov, I. Lapikov, N. Mozdiukova, K. Golovko.
The Kingdom of Women (1967)
Prod. Mosfilm; dir. A. Saltykov. sc. Y. Nagibin. ph. G. Tzekavy, V. Yakushev. des. E. Svidetelev. mus. A. Heshpay; players: R. Markova, N. Sazonova, S. Zhgun, A. Doronina, V. Stolbova.
The Director (1969)
Prod. Mosfilm; dir. A. Saltykov; sc. Y. Nagibin; ph. G. Tzekavy; des. S. Volkov; mus. A. Heshpay; players: N. Gubenko, S. Zhgun, B. Kudryavtzev, V. Sedov, A. Eliseev, V. Daglish.
And There Was an Evening and a Morning (1971)
Prod. Mosfilm; dir. A. Saltykov; sc. E. Volodarsky; ph. G. Tzekavy, V. Yakushev; des. E. Svidetelev; mus. A. Heshpai; players: M. Golubovich, B. Kudryavtzev, Y. Solomin.

Bolotbek Shamshiev
b. 1941 in Kirghizia. Graduated from the VGIK as a director.
Acted
The Heat (1963)
Short films
Manaschi (1966); *The Herdsman* (1967)
Feature films
The Gunshot at the Mountain Pass (1969)
Prod. Kirghizfilm and Kazakhfilm; dir. B. Shamshiev; sc. A. Tarazi, B. Shamshiev; ph. M. Turatbekov; mus. D. Ter-Tatevosyan; players: S. Chokmorov, B. Kadykeeva, S. Dzhumadylov.

Eldar Shengelaya
b. 1933 in Georgia. Graduated from the VGIK as a director (1958).
Short film
Mikela (one episode from *Pages of the Past*), 1964. Prod. Gruzia-Film; dir. and sc. E. Shengelaya; ph. A. Rekhviashvili; des. K. Lebanidze; mus. I. Gedzhadze; players: G. Tkabladze, Z. Kvefenchkhiladze, M. Khvitia.
Feature films
Assistant director to A. Sakharov, *The Legend of the Ice Heart* (1957); *A Snow Fairy-Tale* (1959).
White Caravan (1963, with T. Meliava)
Prod. Gruzia-Film; dir. E. Shengelaya, T. Meliava; sc. M. Eliozishvili; ph. G. Kalatozishvili, L. Kalashnikov; des. D. Takayshvili, K. Lebanidze; mus. I. Gedzhadze; players: S. Bagashvili, A. Shengelaya, I. Kakhiani, G. Kikadze, M. Eliozishvili.
The Unusual Exhibition (1969)
Prod. Gruzia-Film; dir. E. Shengelaya; sc. R. Gabriadze. ph. L. Kalashnikov.
Love, Dagger and Treason (1970)
Prod. Gruzia-Film; dir. E. Shengelaya; sc. R. Gabriadze; ph. G. Kalatozishvili; players: G. Lordkipanidze, V. Chkheidze.

Georgi Shengelaya
b. 1937 in Georgia. Graduated from the VGIK as a director.
Acted
Our Courtyard (1957); *Otar's Widow* (1958); *The Times Are Different Now* (1966).
Short films
Pirosmani (1960);
Allaverdoba (1962–7)

Prod. Gruzia-Film; dir. E. Shengelaya; sc. E. Shengelaya, R. Inanishvili; ph. A. Rekhviashvili.
Reward (1964) (one episode from *The Pages of the Past*)
Prod. Gruzia-Film; dir. and sc. G. Shengelaya; ph. I. Amasyski; des. A. Makarov; mus. F. Glonti; players: S. Takayshvili, B. Goginava.
Feature films
He Did Not Want To Kill (1968)
Prod. Gruzia-Film; dir. G. Shengelaya; sc. G. Asatiani, G. Shengelaya; ph. G. Kalatozishvili, I. Amasyski; des. V. Arabidze, R. Maharadze; players: A. Gabechava, M. Abazadze, G. Kavtaradze, L. Abashidze.
Pirosmani (1971)
Prod. Gruzia-Film; dir. G. Shengelaya; sc. E. Akhvlediani, G. Shengelaya; ph. A. Rekhviashvili, K. Opryatin, D. Margiev; des. A. Varazishvili, V. Arabidze; mus. N. Gabunia; players: A. Varazi, G. Alexsandriya, A. Rekhviashvili, D. Abashidze, Z. Kapianidze.

Larissa Shepitko
b. 1939 in the Ukraine. Graduated from the VGIK as a director (1963). A pupil of A. Dovzhenko.
Short films
The Blind Cook (stud. work); *Living Water* (stud. work); *The Homeland of Electricity* (1968, documentary).
Feature films
Heat (1963)
Prod. Kirghizfilm; dir. L. Shepitko; sc. I. Olshansky, I. Povolotskaya, L. Shepitko, S. Lungin, I. Nusinov; ph. Y. Sokol, V. Arkhangelsky; des. A. Makarov; mus. R. Ledenev; players: B. Shamshiev, N. Zhanturin, K. Yusupdzhanova.

Young Soviet Film Makers

Wings (1966)
Prod. Mosfilm; dir. L. Shepitko; sc. V. Yezhov, N. Ryazantseva; des. I. Plastinkin; mus. R. Ledenev; players: M. Bulgakova, P. Krymov, J. Bolotova, N. Grabbe.
You and I (1971)
Prod. Mosfilm; dir. L. Shepitko; sc. G. Shpalikov; ph. A. Knyazhinsky; des. A. Boym; mus. R. Ledenev; players: Y. Vizbor, B. Akhmadulina, L. Dyachkov.

Gennadi Shpalikov
b. 1937. Graduated from the VGIK as a scriptwriter.
Scripts
I Am Twenty;
I Walk About Moscow;
I Am From Childhood;
You And Me
Feature film
A Long Happy Life (1966)

Vassili Shukshin
b. 1929 in Siberia. Graduated from the VGIK as a director. Writer, actor, scriptwriter.
Acted
Two Fyodors; We, Two Men; The Golden Train; When The Trees Grew Tall; Alenka; The Journalist; By The Lake, etc.
Feature films
There Was A Lad (1964)
Prod. Gorky Studios; dir. and sc. V. Shukshin; ph. V. Ginzburg; des. A. Vagichev; mus. P. Chekalov; players: L. Kuravlev, L. Alexsandrova, L. Burkova, R. Grigorieva, N. Sazonova.
Your Son and Brother (1966)
Prod. Gorky Studios; dir. and sc. V. Shukshin; ph. V. Ginzburg; des. A. Vagichev; players: V. Sanaev, L. Kuravlev.

Strange People (1970)
Prod. Gorky Studios; dir. and sc. V. Shukshin; ph. V. Ginzburg; des. I. Bakhmetiev; mus. K. Khachaturyan; players: Y. Yevstigneev, L. Fedoseeva, Y. Lebedev, G. Bulkina, K. Kozlenkova, N. Smirnov, K. Volkova, M. Shukshina, V. Sanaev, H. Sanaeva, N. Sazonova, P. Krymov.

Andrei Tarkovsky
b. 1932 in Moscow. Graduated from the VGIK as a director.
Short film
The Steam-Roller and the Violin (1961)
Prod. Mosfilm; dir. A. Tarkovsky; sc. A. Mikhalkov-Konchalovsky, A. Tarkovsky; ph. V. Yusov; des. S. Agoyan; mus. V. Ovchinnikov; players: I. Fomchenko, V. Zamansky.
Feature films
Ivan's Childhood (1962)
Prod. Mosfilm; dir. A. Tarkovsky; sc. V. Bogomolov, M. Papava; ph. V. Yusov; des. Y. Chernyaev; mus. V. Ovchinnikov; players: N. Burlyaev, V. Zubkov, V. Malyavina, Y. Zharikov.
Andrei Rublev (1966) Released 1971
Prod. Mosfilm; dir. A. Tarkovsky; sc. A. Tarkovsky; A. Mikhalkov-Konchalovsky; ph. V. Yusov; des. E. Chernyaev. I. Novoderezhkin, S. Voronkov; mus. V. Ovchinnikov; players: N. Burlyaev, A. Solonitsyn, R. Bykov.
Solaris (1972)
Prod. Mosfilm; dir. A. Tarkovsky; sc. A. Tarkovsky; ph. V. Yusov; des. U. Novoderezhkin; players: D. Banionis, N. Grinko, S. Paradzhanov, N. Bondarchuk.

Raymondas Vabalas
b. 1937 in Lithuania. Graduated from the VGIK as a director.

Filmographies

Feature films
Cannonade (1962, with A. Zhebrunas; released 1964). Prod. Lithuanian Film Studio (Vilnius); dir. R. Vabalas, A. Zhebrunas; sc. V. Rimkyavichus; ph. Y. Gritsius; des. A. Zavisha, P. Klishute; mus. E. Balsis; players: E. Pleshkite, S. Petronaytis, V. Murashka, S. Yukna, R. Butkyavichus, B. Babkauskas.
Footsteps in the Night (1963)
Prod. Lithuanian Film Studio; dir. R. Vabalas; sc. V. Mozurunas; ph. Y. Gritsius; des. A. Zavisha, I. Chuplis, V. Bimbayde, E. Emma; mus. E. Balsis; players: I. Rigertas, P. Stepanovichus, V. Tomkus, T. Sharfshteynas, S. Krasauskas, I. Miltinis, G. Vantzavichus.
March, March, Boom-Boom-Boom! (1964)
Prod. Lithuanian Film Studio; dir. R. Vabalas; sc. G. Kanovich, I. Rudas, R. Vabalas; ph. D. Pechura; des. I. Chuplis, V. Dorrer; mus. B. Gorbulskis, I. Chuplis, V. Dorrer; players: L. Stanavichus, V. Yatautis, B. Zhibayte, D. Banenis, G. Gokushayte, G. Karka.
Only Fuehrer is Missing (1965, documentary);
Stairs to the Sky (1966)
Prod. Lithuanian Film Studio; dir. R. Vabalas; sc. M. Slutskis; ph. Y. Gritsius; des. I. Chuplis; players: G. Balandite, A. Ionikas, V. Bledis, I. Gerasimavichute.

Otar Yoseliani
b. 1934 in Georgia. Graduated from the VGIK as a director. Before graduated at the Tbilisi Conservatoire as conductor. Trained as painter and graphic artist. Two years at Moscow University.
Short films
The Watercolour (1958); *Song About A Flower* (1959); *Cast Iron* (1964, documentary).
Feature films
April (1961; unreleased);

When Leaves Fall (1967)
Prod. Gruzia-Film; dir. O. Yoseliani; sc. A. Chichinadze; ph. A. Maysuradze; des D. Eristavi; players: R. Georgobiani, M. Kartzivadze, G. Kharabadze.
Day After Day (1970)

Vadim Yusov
b. 1929 in Moscow. Graduated from the VGIK as a cameraman (1958).
Shot
The Steam-Roller and the Violin (1961); *Ivan's Childhood* (1962); *I Walk About Moscow* (1963); *Andrei Rublev* (1966); *Cheer Up!* (1969); *Solaris* (1972).

Vitautas Zhalakyavichus
b. 1930 in Lithuania. Graduated from the VGIK as a director (1958).
Short films
A Drowned Man (1956); *While There Is Still Time* (1957);
The Living Heroes (1960) (one episode)
Prod. Lithuanian Film Studio; dir. and sc. V. Zhalakyavichus, A. Chekuolis (co-sc.); ph. A. Motzkus; des. M. Bulaka, A. Zhebrunas; mus. E. Balsis; players: L. Malashazhkas, V. Tauyanskis, A. Gabrenas, S. Kosmauskas.
Feature films
Adam Wants To Be A Man (1959)
Prod. Lithuanian Film Studio; dir. and sc. V. Zhalakyavichus, V. Sirios Gira (co-sc.); ph. A. Motzkus; des. A. Nichus; mus. E. Balsis; players: V. Puodzhukaytis, A. Boyarchute, S. Petronaytis, I. Miltinis, V. Bledis.
The Chronicle of One Day (1964)
Prod. Lithuanian Film Studio; dir. and sc. Zhalakyavichus; ph. A. Araminas; des. A. Nichus;

Young Soviet Film Makers

mus. E. Grig, E. Balsis; players: B. Babkauskas, I. Dmitriev, A. Masulis, E. Zhebertavichute, I. Ozerov.
Nobody Wanted to Die (1966)
Prod. Lithuanian Film Studio; dir. and sc. Zhalakyavichus; ph. Y. Gritsius; des. V. Kalinauskas, A. Nichus, V. Bimbayte; mus. A. Apanavichus; players: K. Vitkus, R. Adomaytis, I. Budraytis, A. Masulis, B. Oya, E. Shulgayte, D. Banionis, V. Artmane, D. Bukayte, A. Shurna.

Arunas Zhebrunas
b. 1931 in Lithuania. In 1955 graduated from the Institute of Art, in Vilnius as architect. From 1955 worked as designer.
Short films
The Last Shot (1960, one episode from 'Living Heroes') Prod. Lithuanian Film Studio; dir. A. Zhebrunas; sc. G. Chablyavichus; ph. Y. Gritsius; des. M. Bulaka, A. Zhebrunas; mus. E. Balsis; players: J. Yakelaytite, B. Babkauskas.
Feature films
The Last Day of the School Holiday (1964); *Cannonade* (1962) with R. Vabalas (see Vabalas); *The Black Procession* (1964, documentary);
The Girl and the Echo (1965)
Prod. Lithuanian Film-Studio; dir. and sc. A. Zhebrunas, Y. Nagibin, A. Chernenko (co-sc.); ph. Y. Gritsius; players: L. Braknite.
The Little Prince (1967)
Prod. Lithuanian Film-Studio; dir. and sc. A. Zhebrunas; ph. A. Digimas; players: E. Mikalunas, D. Banionis, O. Koberidze.
The Beautiful Girl (1969)
Prod. Lithuanian Film-Studio; dir. A. Zhebrunas; sc. Y. Yakovlev; ph. A. Motzkus; des. A. Nichus, V. Vilimene; mus. V. Ganelin; players: I. Mitzkite, A. Zhadeykite, S. Martinson, A. Samukas.

13 Selected Bibliography

Actors of Soviet Cinema, numbers 1–6, Iskusstvo, Moscow–Leningrad, 1964–70.
Dictionary of Cinema, 2 vols., 'Soviet Encyclopaedia', Moscow, 1966–70.
Ekran, Iskusstvo, Moscow, 1964–70.
Essays on the History of Soviet Cinema, 3 vols., Iskusstvo Kino, Moscow, 1957–71.
Hibbin, Nina, *Eastern Europe, an illustrated guide*, A. Zwemmer Ltd–A.S. Barnes & Co., London–New York.
History of Soviet Cinema 1917–67, 4 vols., Iskusstvo, Moscow, 1966–70.
Houston, Penelope, *The Contemporary Cinema*, Penguin Books, London, 1963.
Iskusstvo Kino, Moscow, 1957–71.
Leyda, Jay, *Kino, A History of the Russian and Soviet Film*, George Allen & Unwin Ltd., London, 1960.
Macheret, A., *Art Tendencies in Soviet Cinema*, Iskusstvo, Moscow, 1963.
Problems of Cinema Art, numbers 1–12, Nauka, Moscow, 1957–70.
Short History of Soviet Cinema 1917–67, Iskusstvo, Moscow, 1969.
Sovetski Ekran, 1958–71.
Soviet Feature Films, catalogue in 4 vols., Iskusstvo, Moscow, 1963–68.
Soviet Film 1957–71.
Vladimirova, Z., *Igor Ilyinsky*, Iskusstvo, Moscow, 1967.
Weisfeld, I., *Tomorrow and Today*, Iskusstvo, Moscow, 1968.
Young Soviet Directors, Iskusstvo, Leningrad–Moscow, 1962.
Yurenev, R., *The Soviet Comedy*, Nauka, Moscow, 1964.

General Index

adventure films 24, 51, 60, 72, 95
allegories 32, 99
artistic life: as subject of films 21, 33–5, 43, 46, 49, 72–3
avant-garde 19

Belgrade Festival 35
biographical films 18, 21, 68, 69
bureaucracy: oppressiveness of 17; satirised in films 36–7, 51, 56

Cannes Festival 20, 33, 70, 83, 87
Central Asian Republics: cinema in 9, 22, 91–101
childhood 27, 82, 96
children's films 41, 69
cinéma d'auteur 19, 50
cinema of images 32
circus: elements of in films 51, 53, 57, 59
Civil War 17, 23, 28; as featured in films 27, 29, 41, 49, 60, 66, 67
colour films 19, 20, 28, 32, 35, 80, 83, 88, 99, 100
comedy 22, 32, 51–9, 60, 68, 69, 74; children's 41; musical 53; 'new' comedy 52; political 20, 38, 51, 66, 80; slapstick and eccentric 51, 56
commercial cinema 41, 60–2, 65, 66, 70, 72, 77, 78, 84
conformity: rejection of 23, 27–32
contemporary society: avoidance of controversial subjects in 32, 36; features on 19, 36, 52, 70, 99; interest in 27, 41, 74; *see also* youth
control over films 52, 60; relaxation of 31
Cracow Festival 45, 74, 91
creativity, individual *see* self-expression

directors: individualists 22, 74, 77; prizes 60; working conditions 60
documentaries 61, 65, 69, 70–1, 77, 81, 91, 94; in style of 74, 94
Dovzhenko Studio 32, 104
dreams and reality: dichotomy as portrayed in films 28, 46, 73

education: treatment of problems in film 19

fantasy 29, 74
FEX group (factory of the eccentric actor) 29
'fighting anthologies' 53
Filma 65
First World War 47, 60, 69
folklore and folk festivals 32, 65, 66, 75, 77, 87–90, 93
Frankfurt Festival 92

George Sadoul prize 74
Georgian cinema 9, 22, 65–9, 70–80
Glavkinoprokat (State Distributor of films) 60
Gorky Film Studios, Moscow 44, 77, 104, 105
Goskinprom Studio 65, 68
Gruzia Film Studios 70, 77, 104

hidden camera: use of 43, 73, 74
horror films 18

ideological films *see* propaganda
'independent cinema' 29
industrialisation 17, 41, 68
intelligentsia, Soviet 20, 67
Izvestia 24

Karlovy Vary International Film Festival 81
Keystone Cops 51
kolkhoz (collective farm) 17, 36; as depicted in films 41, 52, 53, 68, 70, 91
Kommissarzhevskaya Theatre 57
Krokodil 42

LEF (Left Front of the Arts) 30
Lenfilm Studio 49, 77, 104, 105
Leningrad Bolshoi Drama Theatre 30
Leningrad Polytechnical Institute 42
Leningrad Theatre of Comedy 58
Lithuanian Film Studio 81–5, 104
Locarno International Film Festival 48, 83, 87, 96
love themes 19, 42–3, 44, 60, 85, 96, 98

Mar-del-Plata Festival 32, 87
melodrama 66, 67
MHAT (Moscow Art Theatre) 23, 57
Moldova Film Studio 87, 104
Moscow University 61, 73
Mosfilm Studios 69, 74, 78, 92, 104, 105
musical accompaniment 56, 58, 75, 90, 91, 92, 93; musical acts 53, 69; original score 54
musical films 53, 69

nature, as depicted in films 28, 30, 65, 68, 77, 92–5
neo-realism: Italian 20, 74; Soviet ('kitchen sink' films) 29
newsreels: cameramen 24, 43; influence in film-making 65, 69, 81; use in film-making 85
Novy Mir 49

Oberhausen Film Festival 74, 93
official line 18, 84; under Stalin 52–3, 67–9, 81–2, 91
Olympians, the 24

Pathé 65
political climate: influence of 17,

Index

18, 48, 51–4, 61–9
'positive heroes' 53
propaganda: use in films 17–18, 24, 27, 32, 52–3, 60, 69, 70
psychology, female 20, 45
purges 17
purdah: importance in Azerbaidzhan cinema 70

RAPP (Russian Association of Proletarian Writers) 52
realism: dogmatic 21; in films 20, 88; reaction against 23, 27–32, 41; social 9, 18, 36, 52
religious subjects: treatment in films 29, 33, 66, 67, 71–2
revolution: Georgian (1905) 66; Russian 17, 27, 29, 41, 52, 60
Riga Film Studio 42, 104
romantic films 20, 29, 32, 66, 83–4, 88, 96
'Rosta Windows' 67
rural life: as depicted in films 20, 36, 41, 50, 65, 69, 71, 75–7

satire 20, 36, 38, 51, 53, 54, 56, 66
Second World War 17–18, 24, 43, 53, 60, 81, 91
self-expression 23, 30–2, 98; stifling of 17, 60; in young generation 18, 27, 32, 42
Selznick prize 28
serial features 24, 65
sex films 18
Shchukin Theatre School 30, 42, 59
'shelved' films 9, 20, 22, 36, 80
Soviet Film Weeks 9, 49, 50, 96
'Sovremennik' Youth Theatre, Moscow 30, 47, 61
space exploration 28
sports films 60, 61, 78
'spy films' 17
Stalinism 17–18, 52, 67–9; pseudohistorical films 17, 24, 68–9;

reaction against 18, 24, 77, 81; see also realism: social
State Commission (censor) 60, 69, 80; see also 'shelved' films
State Committee of Cinematography 60
Sverdlovsk Theatre 35

Tbilisi Music School 73
Theatre of Satire 59
thrillers 77, 82
tragi-comic films 54–5, 73, 77
tribes: as subjects of films 66, 88

Vakhtangov Theatre 48, 62
Venice Festival 19, 28, 49
VGIK (All-Union State Cinematography Institute) 23–4, 27, 36, 38, 44, 73, 74; graduates of 19, 22, 32, 41, 46, 47, 50, 71, 73, 77, 82, 87, 91, 93, 96; teachers at 18, 44, 50, 77
village life see rural life

war: as theme of films 19, 20, 44, 47–8; see also individual wars
Westerns, style of 66
working-class life: films about 39, 41

Yalta Studio 32, 104
youth, contemporary: generation gap 38, 73; theme in films 19, 20, 74, 78, 98

Index of Names

Abesadze, Otar 77, 106, 108, 109
Abuladze, Tengiz 21, 24, 32, 61, 70, 106, 107
Agishev, Odelsha 22, 95, 96, 98, 109
Akbarkhodzhaev, K. 108
Akhmadulina, Bella 39
Akhundov, Mirza 70
Akhvlediani, Erlom 72
Akimov, Nikolai 58
Akmukhamedov, S. 100
Alexandrov, Grigori 24, 52, 53
Alov, Alexander 9, 19, 20, 106, 107
Amushukeli, Vassili 65
Antipenko, A. 32
Araminas, Algirdas 83, 85, 108, 109
Aribidze, V. 73
Arnstam, L. 24
Arsenov, Pavel 45, 77, 107, 108, 109
Asatiani, George 71
Aytmatov, Chingiz 28
Aznavour, Charles 56

Banionis, Donatas 28
Barnet, Boris 23, 51
Barsky 65, 66
Basov, V. 24
Batalov 61
Bek-Nazarov, Amo 66, 69
Berishvili, Zakhari 66
Blumental-Tamarina, Maria 51
Bogin, Mikhail 20, 42–4, 107, 108, 110
Bogomolov, V. 43
Bondarchuk, Sergei 19, 20, 31, 106, 107, 108
Bratkauskas, Balis 81, 82, 106
Bronstein, Y. 91
Brylska, Barbara 95
Bulgakova, Maya 39
Bykov, Rolan 56, 61, 107

Chaplin, Charlie 56
Chavchavadze, Ilya 75
Chebotaryov, V. 106
Chekhov, Anton 20, 22, 24, 29, 31, 61
Cherniaev, Yevgeni 35
Chiaureli, Mikhail 66, 67, 68, 106
Chkheidze, Rezo 24, 70, 106, 107

Chubinidze, Toma 68
Chukhrai, Grigori 18, 19, 23, 106, 107
Chulukin, Yuri 42, 54, 106
Churikova, Inna 49, 61
Chursina, Ludmila 48, 62

Danelia, Georgi 9, 19, 22, 54, 56, 70, 78, 80, 106, 107, 108, 110
Demidova, Alla 62
Derbenev, Vadim 87, 106, 108, 111
Digmelov, Alexander 65, 66
Disney, Walt 56
Dmitriev, A. 51
Dolidze, Siko 66, 68
Doronin, M. 91
Dostoyevsky, Fyodor 20, 31, 61
Dovlatyan, Frunze 70, 107
Dovzhenko, Alexander 9, 18, 21, 24, 38, 73
Drutse, Ion 87
Dunayevas, F. 81
Dunayevsky 53
Dzhavakhishvili, M. 68

Eisenstein, Sergei 9, 18, 20, 24, 29, 53, 69, 70, 91, 106
Esadze, S. 65
Esakia, Leo 66

Fainzimmer, Alexander 106
Fatkhullin, Dilshat 22, 95, 96, 98
Fedotovas, V. 81
Fernandel 59
Fetin, Vladimir 42, 47–8, 107, 108, 111
Filippov, Sergei 58–9
Freilikh, O. 91
Fyodorova, Victoria 42

Gabriadze, Rezo 54, 112
Gabrilovich, Yevgeni 49
Ganiev, N. 91

125

Young Soviet Film Makers

Gardin, Vladimir 23, 24
Garin, Erast 57-8
Gaydai, Leonid 54, 56, 106, 107, 108
Gazhiu, Valeri 87, 107, 108, 112
Gedris, Marionas 81, 82, 83, 106, 112
Gelovani, Mikhail 66
Gerassimov, S. 24
Gertel, K. 91
Gogitidze, G. 65
Gogoberidze, Lana 107
Gogol, Nikolai 21, 32, 57
Gozzi, Carlo 77
Grigoriev, Yevgeni 41, 112
Grin, Alexander 45
Groshev, Professor A. N. 24

Heifitz, Josef 19, 20, 43, 61, 106, 107
Henry, O. 54
Hitler, Adolf 17, 81

Ilyenko, Yuri 20, 21, 22, 32, 61, 107, 108, 113
Ilyinsky, Igor 51, 54, 56-7
Ishmukhamedov, Elier 22, 60, 95, 96, 98, 107, 108, 113
Ivanovsky, Alexander 52

Kalantar, L. 69
Kalatozishvili, Georgi 77, 108, 113
Kalatozov, Mikhail 18, 19, 53, 61, 67, 68, 73, 106, 107
Kalik, Mikhail 19, 87, 106
Kandelaki, Gela 77, 113
Karasik, Yuli 22, 108
Karsakbaev, Abdulla 100-1, 107, 113
Kazansky, G. 106
Kazbegi, A. 66
Kerbabaev, Berdy 99
Khamraev, Ali 95, 98-9, 107, 108, 114
Khanzhonkov, Alexander 68

Khmelik, Alexander 46
Khodzhaev, N. 91
Khokhlova, Alexandra 23
Khrushchev, Nikita 20, 37, 41, 52
Khutsiev, Marlen 9, 19-20, 22, 23, 41, 47, 49, 74, 98, 106, 107
Kldiashvili, David 77
Klepikov, Yuri 36
Klimas, G. 81
Klimov, Elem 36-8, 54, 56, 60, 61, 107, 108, 114
Klimov, Herman 61
Kobakhidze, Mikhail 22, 56, 71, 74-5, 107, 108, 115
Kokochashvili, Merab 71, 73, 75-7, 106, 107, 115
Komarov, S. 51
Korablyov, Yevgeni 35
Korchagin, M. 24
Koshevorova, Nadezda 106
Kozintsev, Grigori 19, 30, 47, 62, 107, 108
Ktorov, Anatoli 51
Kubrick, Stanley 28
Kulagin, Leonid 30
Kuleshov, Lev 9, 23, 24, 29, 51, 67
Kupchenko, Irina 30
Kuznetsov, Anatoli 49
Kveselava, Alexander 21, 32

Lamorisse, Albert 19, 47
Lemm, Stanislaw 28
Lenartas, Y. 81
Lenin, Vladimir Ilyich Ulyanov 17, 19
Leonidov, Leonid 23
Lermontov 66
Letuvaite, A. 81
Lipman, Jerzy 44
London, Jack 24
Lotyanu, Emil 88, 107, 108, 115
Lubimov, Pavel 19, 20, 42, 44-6, 106, 107, 108, 115
Lukov, L. 91
Lunacharsky 23

Lungin, Semyon 36, 38
Lysenko, Vadim 87, 107, 116
Lysenko, Yuri 106

Makarov, Georgi 66, 68
Managadze, Shota 70
Mansurov, Bulat 99-100, 107, 108, 116
Mardzhanishvili, Kote 66, 67
Martirosyan, A. 69
Masina, Giulietta 49
Matisse, Henri 19
Mayakovsky 67
Mdivani, G. 66
Medvedkin, Alexander 52
Meliava, Tamaz 73, 107, 116
Meyerhold, Vsevolod 23, 57
Mikhalkov-Konchalovsky, Andron 9, 19, 20, 27, 28-32, 33, 35, 36, 61, 107, 108, 116
Milus, P. 81
Minervin, A. 69
Mironer, Felix 106
Mironov, Andrei 59, 62
Mitskite, Inga 84
Mitta, Alexander 41, 42, 46-7, 54, 106, 107, 108, 117
Mokicz, Leonard 44

Nagibin, Yuri 41
Narliev, K. 100
Naumov, Vladimir 9, 19, 20, 47, 106, 107
Navoi, Alisher 99
Nikulin, Yuri 56, 59
Ninoshvili, E. 65, 68
Nova, Sagat 21
Novoderezhkin, Ippolit 35
Nusinov, Ilya 36, 38

Oganesyan, Georgi 55, 107
Okeev, Tolomush 22, 92-3, 107, 108, 117
Orlova, Lubov 53, 58
Osepyan, Mark 41, 107, 118

Ostashenko, E. 28
Ovchinnikov, Vyacheslav 35

Palavandishvili, S. 68
Panfilov, Gleb 9, 42, 48-9, 54, 60, 107, 108, 118
Papanov, Anatoli 61
Paradzhanov, Sergei 20, 21, 23, 28, 32, 61, 107, 108
Pasternak, Boris 17-18
Perestiani, Ivan 24, 51, 66, 67, 68
Petrov, Andrei 54
Pinkauskaite, P. 81
Pipinashvili, Konstantin 69
Pironais 65
Pirosmanishvili, Niko 67, 72-3
Platonov, Andrei 77, 100
Popov, Alexei 51
Preobrazhenskaya, Olga 23
Proklova, Helena 46, 47
Pronin, Vassili 41, 107
Protazanov, Yakov 9, 29, 51, 91
Pshavela, Vazha 21, 32
Ptushko, Alexander 106
Pudovkin, Vsevolod 9, 18, 23, 24, 70
Push 67
Pyriev, Ivan 17, 20, 52

Rachunas, A. 81
Raizman, Yuli 19, 106
Raksa, Pola 44
Razumny, Alexander 106
Reisz, Karel 41
Roach, Hal 51
Romm, Mikhail 19, 50, 77, 106
Rondeli, David 66, 68, 69
Roshal, Grigory 24, 44, 58
Rostotsky, S. 44
Rouch, Jean 66
Ryazanov, Eldar 54, 55, 107
Rytsarev, Boris 106

Saint-Exupéry, Antoine de 19, 83
Saltykov, Alexei 36, 41, 46, 106,

Index

107, 108, 118
Samoilova, Tatyana 18, 61
Samsonov, S. 24
Sanishvili, N. 69
Savchenko, I. 24
Savelieva 61
Savina, Iya 61–2
Sergachev, Victor 30
Seifullina, Lidia 47–8
Shamshiev, Bolot 22, 38, 91, 93–5, 108, 118
Shapiro, Mikhail 106
Sharif-Zade 70
Shengelaya, Eldar 70, 71, 73, 107, 108, 119
Shengelaya, Georgi 70, 71–3, 74, 107, 108, 119
Shengelaya, Nikolai 67, 68, 71
Shepitko, Larissa 9, 19, 22, 38–9, 92, 93, 107, 108, 119
Shirvanidze, Alexander 69
Shklovsky, Victor 67, 72
Shmein 57
Shostakovich, Dmitri 9
Shpalikov, Gennadi 54, 120
Shukshin, Vassili 42, 49–50, 54, 107, 108, 120

Shvante, Jim 68
Shveitser, Mikhail 22, 108
Slutskyus, Mikolas 85
Smirnitsky, Valentin 42
Smoktunovsky, Innokenti 19, 20, 31, 55, 61
Sokol, Yuri 38, 47
Solonitsyn, Anatoli 35
Stalin, Josef 17, 57, 69
Stanislavsky, Konstantin 23
Stykovsky, N. 51

Talankin, Igor 19, 21, 78, 106, 108
Tarkovsky, Andrei 9, 19, 20, 23, 27–8, 33–5, 106, 107, 108, 120
Tillier, Claude 54, 80
Tisse, E. 24
Todorovsky, Pyotr 20, 107
Tolstoy, Leo 31, 78
Trauberg 30
Trifonov, Y. 100
Trotsky, Leon 17
Tsereteli, G. 66
Tsutsunava, Alexander 65, 66
Tumanishvili, I. 69
Turatbekov 95

Turgenev, Ivan 20, 30, 31
Tyszkiewicz, Beata 30

Unt, Mati 85
Urbansky, Yevgeni 41
Urusevsky, Sergei 18, 19
Usoltsev-Garf, A. 91
Utyosov, Leonid 53

Vabalas, Raimondas 84–5, 106, 120
Vachnadze, Nato 67, 71
Vaichkus, I. 81
Vakhtangov, Yevgeni 23
Varazishvili, Avtandil 73
Vasiliev, Georgi 24, 58
Vasiliev, Sergei 24, 58
Vengerov 106
Verigo-Darovsky, F. 91
Vertinskaya, Anastasia 61, 62
Vertinsky, Alexander 62
Vertov, Dziga 9, 18, 30
Vidugiris, A. 91
Vogel, Vladimir 23
Voinich, Lilian 66
Volodin, Alexander 37, 46
Voronkov, Stepan 35

Wajda 20, 27
Wolyniec, Roman 44

Yarmatov, K. 91
Yarvet, Yuri 28
Yefremov, Oleg 47, 56, 61
Yermolinsky, Sergei 46
Yevtushenko, Yevgeni 39
Yoseliani, Otar 9, 22, 71, 73–4, 77, 107, 108, 121
Yusov, Vadim 19, 22, 27–8, 33, 54, 78, 80, 121
Yutkevich, Sergei 53, 62, 73

Zabozlaev, S. 66
Zakariadze, Sergo 68
Zakrutkin, Vitali 77
Zarkhi, Alexander 107
Zarkhi, N. 24
Zguridi, Alexander 95
Zhalakyavichus, Vitautas 60–1, 81, 82, 106, 107, 121
Zharov, Mikhail 51
Zhdanov 9
Zhebrunas, Arunas 81, 82, 83–4, 106, 107, 122
Zhelyabuzhsky, Yuri 24, 67

For Product Safety Concerns and Information please contact our EU representative GPSR@taylorandfrancis.com
Taylor & Francis Verlag GmbH, Kaufingerstraße 24, 80331 München, Germany

www.ingramcontent.com/pod-product-compliance
Lightning Source LLC
Chambersburg PA
CBHW061418300426
44114CB00015B/1985